The Thornhill 360, one of the most
beautiful and iconic skate photos of all time.
Laura Thornhill, skater. *Warren Bolster.*

URETHANE REVOLUTION

The Birth of
SKATE
SAN DIEGO 1975

JOHN O'MALLEY

THE
History
PRESS

Published by The History Press
Charleston, SC
www.historypress.com

Front cover: Bobby Piercy. *Warren Bolster.*
Back cover, top: Dave Dominey. *Lance Smith.*
Back cover, inset: Laura Thornhill. *Warren Bolster.*

First published 2019

Manufactured in the United States

ISBN 9781467139908

Library of Congress Control Number: 2018960984

Notice: The information in this book is true and complete to the best of our knowledge. It is offered without guarantee on the part of the author or The History Press. The author and The History Press disclaim all liability in connection with the use of this book.

For
Joe Twyford
whose Deep Listening
was a superpower.

Chris Strople captured
in strobe on the clear
plastic Firestone Ramp.
Warren Bolster.

FOR LISTENING

Cindy, Di, Betsy, TSJ, Kennedy, MAC

THANKS AND ACKNOWLEDGEMENTS

(in no particular order)
Dan Lefkowitz
Margaret M. Whitehead
Don Sheridan
Ding and Judy Fix
Betsey Binkley Gordon
Di Dootson
Jane Rogers
Janet & Mike Tremonte
Warren Bolster
Cindy Berryman
Dave Dash
Thomas W. Hazlett
Gary Holterman
(This was all your fault—we both know this.)
Lance Smith
Bill Bahne
Bob Bahne
Charlie Nelson
Sally Ann Miller
Noel Korman
Ann Myeroff
Tommy T
Adam Dabonka
Wes Humpston
Stan Strocher
Milk SoNo
Laura Thornhill

VERY, VERY, VERY, BIG THANKS TO THE PHOTOGRAPHERS FOR THEIR SPECTACULAR CONTRIBUTIONS:

Warren Bolster Estate
Lance Smith
Larry Balma
Richard "Slick" Dowdy
Art Brewer
Glen Miyoda
John Malvino
Di Dootson archive
Laura Thornhill Archive
Tracker Trucks Archive
Jim Goodrich

Special thanks to Tracker Trucks for their support. Tracker has a spectacular, 388-page book about its forty-year ride. It's jam-packed with cool photos and stories, and it is one terrific deal; you should tool over to the Tracker website and buy a copy right now. Go ahead, do it now, this will keep.

Note: Some of my photos were smoke damaged a while back, but I decided to run the ones that I loved here anyway.

And finally, I totally hit the EDITOR JACKPOT! with Laurie Krill. Thank you for picking me out of the pile. And thanks to everyone at The History Press who helped bring this book to life.

Tom Sims, longboarding at the Concrete
Wave Skatepark, decades before
longboarding became cool. So, I ask the
question: When did it become okay to
exclude long boards in your skateparks?
Warren Bolster.

CONTENTS

Concrete Wave Skatepark overview.
Warren Bolster.

FOREWORD

If you've never read any of the bits that I publish in the gravity sports rags, you're probably not missing too much. They're usually just my field reports from some collision of idiots. I stay out of the frame and hold the material up to the light for a minute—try to keep my head down.

Don't you hate it when some knob breaks into your stream just to listen to himself talk?

But even worse is the Dry White Toast (DWT) of the Reverential. Recount. Of. Facts.

I can't stand any of that tedious crap.

And unfortunately for me, this sitting down and writing it all out nice, is just a big, big, pain in the ass. I'd rather open up a genuine White Toast Store, where I butter you an artisanal sourdough slice, singed to perfection. You pay me my five bucks and we each go our own way with bellies full and dignity somewhat intact.

And it's not like we haven't worn out some good stretch of this road already with the telling and retelling, ad nauseam, of tales of the excellent Dogtown/Z-Boys skaters. They are our brothers, and we love them. Best crew ever. But it's thrown shade over what is truly the larger story.

And then one day I saw a posting online from a preeminent Dry White Toast guy, stating correctly, that the seventies skate crew—my crew—had done a poor job of telling their story.

And that's what rang my bell.

But shout over decades of fist-pumping Dogtown liturgy?

I'll pass.

And besides…Me? I like a fish story.

But then one day, I caught a glimpse of a fish story where I'm in the frame just an inch and thought…well then…

Now we have a car chase. Or two…

Now we have a plane crash. Or two…

Now we have senior White House staff…

The Mafia…

Fast cars…

A Gypsy fortuneteller…

Naked hippie chicks…

Colombian narcos…

Jacques Cousteau…

And the six-hundred-pound gorilla in the room passing out straws…

Huge piles of blow…

Now…we have a fish story.

So I guess I'm your guy.

Beginning in around 1974, there'd be a convergence of these talented and tangent individuals arriving to take up the Surf Life in Encinitas, California. Some of them would become essential in the creation of our modern-day Skate culture.

I can't explain how it was that these few converged on the same backwater beach town at the same time. But for my part, it went like this…

OPPOSITE, TOP Your Tracker Trucks delivered by handsome hippies, Keith Hagen (*left*) and Lance Smith. © *Larry Balma/Tracker Archive.*

OPPOSITE, BOTTOM Local surfer Deano, waiting for a ride. *Richard Dowdy.*

FLOWERS F S

Early flower power, Encinitas.
Richard Dowdy.

Russ Gosnell skating the Tracker ramp.
© *Lance Smith/Tracker Archive.*

TRAJECTORY (NOUN)

1: The path followed by a projectile flying or an object moving under the action of given forces.
2: A curve or surface cutting a family of curves or surfaces at a constant angle.

I hear those tsks and groans. Yeah that's right, the definition gambit. Lamest opening of 'em all.

Just give me another minute here…

Tony Alva (*right*) and Bruce Logan. Carlsbad
Skatepark, early days. *Warren Bolster*.

THE URETHANE REVOLUTION

The Revolution is over. Skaters won.

Just? Here, step to the window:

Skateboarders gliding by, silently commuting on long, electric sleds.

They're shredding at the skatepark—that you paid for—on comfy, fat, pool boards.

They're going OFF in foul territory right now. Leapfrogging stairways on common popsicle boards—each with its artwork carefully curated. THWACK! Solid landing. Aaaaand…the middle-finger salute going away… FUCK YOU.

Nice touch.

You surrendered—we won.

How'd this all happen?

Around 1973, a guy named Frank Nasworthy discovered these urethane training wheels that were used on beginners' roller skates. They were grippier than the unforgiving composite clay wheels of the day.

Frank bolted them onto his skateboard and bingo! Suction-cup traction like no one had ever imagined possible.

It's in that instant that the skateboard went from a toy with feet of clay to a wall-climbing UFO, screaming at warp speed to the 2020 Olympics.

This would be the Urethane part of it.

The Revolution began when a rift opened in the universe and that centrifugal buzz—heretofore available only through sports like surfing and skiing—came leaking out of the streets. Adrenaline rushing up your road, serotonin dripping down the drive.

And the scales fell from our eyes: *Any paved surface could be ridden.*

And the call went out:

The Rift has opened
God is great
Spread the word

Coincident with the rise of Nasworthy's company Cadillac Wheels, the mid-1970s saw:

- A historic drought in the American Southwest.
- A long, deep, financial recession.
- The nadir of professional surfing.
- Gangsters raid the Central States Teamsters' retirement fund and build themselves a new playground down in sunny Saaaan Dieeeegoooo!

This perfect storm of ill winds was the jet stream of the Revolution.

What'd that look like?

The drought uncovered insanely fun new skating forms like reservoirs and drainage ditches while recession-vacant homes had their swimming pools drained and skated. Our eyes spocked an urban landscape lit up with a million new possibilities.

The Revolution lasted about a year and is bookended by two landmark contests: the Bahne/Cadillac contest held at the Del Mar Fairgrounds in April 1975 and the ABC/Hang Ten World Championships from Carlsbad Skatepark in September 1976.

All the sport's inventions, competitive standards and industry associations would emerge during this year, and nothing's changed much—except that the kids have gotten so much better.

OPPOSITE The view down the slalom ramp at the Bahne/Cadillac skateboard contest. *Bahne Archive.*

Box Canyon kids' race. Looks like a seven-cone course with "catchers" at the end. © *Tracker Archive.*

The feeding frenzy that began in 1975 was just ferocious, and by 1977, billion-dollar annual aggregates were predicted. But that all began to unravel late in 1978 (which I call the Crash of '79).

Why? Market saturation plus a financial and demographic downturn. We'd ridden an XXL wave to the crest and were now sucking straight down the back into the pit.

The fledgling sport skogged into a headwind a dozen years deep that changed it irrevocably.

The demise of the grand, commercial skateparks left a vacancy of vert and precipitated the rise of street skating.

A quick measure of the thing is to trace the arch of *SkateBoarder Magazine*. By 1977, just two years after its launch, the magazine had grown to be a grand 148 ad-packed pages with a readership of 2.1 million per month.

Now there's only about thirteen million teenage boys in the U.S. in 1977, so *SkateBoarder* was generating enough impressions to saturate each one of those groms every six months.

What'd that look like? It was typical for a kid to plaster the walls of his room with posters of sports, Lynda Carter, Farrah Fawcett and their favorite skater girl.

SkateBoarder Magazine's idyllic vision of skateboarding as this explosive, new, surf-centric sport went viral on a global scale.

Memed, at a time when memes came along once a decade, and state-of-the-art office technology was carbon paper.

News directors worldwide, captivated by *SkateBoarder*'s vision, ran features, rocketing the sport to global prominence. All the networks, beginning with ABC, broadcast contest segments of the big events.

Counterculture much?

When bad times and mob money pay for the party, that's fucking counterculture.

Once upon a time we were simply surfing's little brother, but somewhere along the line, skate became the nexus of an entire extreme sports universe. Surfing, snowboarding, wakeboarding, kite boarding—even skiing—all nod inward to skate's primal influence. Professionals practicing any of these sports will skate seriously to train in the off-season.

In 2016, skateboarding became an Olympic sport, and riders broke one hundred miles per hour. Forty-sum years is high time to revisit how it happened, because it was all just so...unlikely.

Carlsbad Moguls. *John O'Malley Archive.*

JUST LIKe In THe MOVIeS

For my part, I was spit out of the mouth of Hell directly into the sweet bosom of Southern California…It's 11:00 a.m. on a fine Friday in July, Hicksville, New York, and I'm already a few hours late to begin my route delivering beer before heading out to my Montauk hideaway to surf for the weekend. A friend's dad hooked me up with this summer job as a driver's helper for a regional beer distributor, despite me being too young to drink or drive—both requisite job duties.

But as I review our route tickets, my Montauk plans are beginning to evaporate. Driver Tommy Kincaid and I have waited all morning just to pull the last and worst route of the week—the eternal plight of the lowest man on the totem pole.

The math on how long it will take us to complete our route of fuck-all delis and bars flung indiscriminately across Nassau and Queens Counties was pretty grim. North Shore to South Shore, an A&P, a bowling alley—the airport for Christ's sake. We could be out there chasing down these ne'er-do-wells and CODs until way after dark.

The guys with seniority and the best routes are already arriving back at the depot and laughing at us because they know that our route is made up mostly of tickets that they'd tossed back into the pile—pain-in-the-ass stops that no one felt like making. I'll be left to find my tent hidden deep in the Shadmore Woods near Ditch Plains in the pitch dark. Always dicey.

But the Hofbrauhaus and strip joints on COD would not be getting their weekend delivery today. And my sweet little tent in the woods would never see me again. Because unbeknownst to me, God has slipped another ticket on top of our pile, and my next stop—and last in the beer business—would be the burn unit at Meadowbrook Hospital.

Our truck is an ancient ten-bay, gas-powered, International Harvester beverage rig that the yard guys have loaded up lopsided, overfilled the gas tank and left for us at the ready spot.

And boy, it looks sloppy as we approach: listing to the right and dripping gas from the spout jutting out from below my door. I smell it bad as I climb up into the cab.

The loading crew punched in every day at 4:00 a.m. and began each workday by religiously cracking a seven-ounce Ballantine pony, which were kept chilled in the fridge courtesy of the company (the seven-ounce size being the only nod to temperance in an age when drinking and driving was totally dismissed for the general public and considered a necessary job skill in this line of work).

For instance, it was an insult to refuse the obligatory shot and a beer when getting your ticket signed at a bar stop. This occurred at a dozen stops a day. Do the math, and it adds up to a complete supply chain of drunks. Another drinking-driver I worked with, O'Leary, was kept on the job despite backing into a Fotomat and tipping it over, Fotomate, as the female attendants were then called, still inside and screaming bloody murder.

Hiccup? Yerrr welllcommme...

The loading ritual of pulling tickets, drinking, loading cases and barrels of beer onto the rigs and drinking, continued all morning, ending this day with our POS truck: the last load of the week on a fine-as-kine Friday in July. Just stack that shit in there and go the fuck home.

On the plus side, the drunker that the loaders got, the worse their math was, so there's a good chance that there would be a few cases of imported Löwenbräus leftover to take with me to Montauk—if we even finished this malignant route by midnight.

We leave the barn the prototypical accident waiting to happen—overloaded, starboard-heavy and dripping a trail of gas on the ground while creeping toward our appointment with a driver in a larger truck, already dead drunk and doing twice the speed limit.

A left and two quick rights puts us on Jericho Turnpike, then westward-ho to our first stop, a dive bar on COD in Queens.

We're pulling slow uphill on Jericho, making maybe ten miles per hour, and as I roll down my window, there's a blur of movement in the opera window behind the driver's head. A huge truck just jumped the grass meridian beside us and is barreling this way at about thirty miles per hours. I was sure he'd kill the guy in back of us and then BAM!!! He rams US in the rear instead. We tilt up onto the right two wheels and I counter by leaning away, but the scale of things is way too out of whack for my skinny body to tip the balance back. Then the right-leaning load shifts, and the rest of the events happen in extra-wide screen, super-slow motion.

The rig rolls over onto its side, tossing a seatbelt-less Tommy Kincaid on top of me and we slide along, passenger-side of the truck facing down.

With the weight of a full-grown man pressing down on me, I brace my forearms above and below the open window to hold myself from being pushed out of the cab and crushed. Sparks fly off the side-view mirror and I think to myself, *It's just like in the movies*. You know, how they put a camera inside the car and roll it over so you get that crazy point of view. It's exactly like that, but here it's almost soft and cushy with the impact of the crash absorbed by the huge mass of the truck and cargo.

As we skid along, Tommy on top of me, the pavement inches from my face, I think to myself: *This fucker's gonna blow.*

And just like dragging a match across the hot asphalt of Jericho Turnpike, the fuel ignites and I'm slammed with a conclusive blast that singes my arms and face with a throaty TWOOSHHHH!!! As we slide gently to a stop, the exterior of the cab is engulfed in flames and fire licks inside through the open window on the floor.

…Just like in the movies.

I right myself fast; the flames outside the cab obscure my view through the windshield, now in a vertical position on my right.

Tommy is wrestling futilely with the driver's door on the ceiling and our only way out. But the frame of the truck has shifted in the crash, and the door is jammed shut.

I hear a woman just outside the truck, screaming: "There's men in there! They're dying!!!"

In my head, I respond, *Fuck there is. I'M in here and I'm just a boy*. As Tommy struggles upside down with the door on the ceiling, I observe that I am now ankle-deep in fire and not experiencing terrible pain. Then I flash back to a short story by this guy who had survived a tiger attack in a bare-handed battle to the death. In his narrative, he recounted that, despite his savage mauling, there wasn't the expected level of pain.

Just like in the tiger story, I thought. Maybe nature buffers us from the final horrors of death. Maybe those slowest springbok that are run down and slaughtered on the veldt are spared terrible pain by some mercy deep within their brain.

Then I lit on the scenes where people scream bloody murder while they're being immolated. This was really, really dire now. And I made the decision that if things got too bad, I'd choose to not live the horrible life now at hand and endure this screaming hell right to the end. And may God damn me there, forever and ever amen.

If you're wondering how all these conversations can blow through your mind in just a moment, so did I, and this is just a portion of them.

Now Tommy braces himself in an upside-down position, blasts the door open using both feet and all his might and scrambles right out.

Every man for himself now.

Next, there's a surge in the flames fueled by the escaping air. Now there's no daylight above me, and the cab's totally engulfed in flames. Tommy got out just in time. Knee-deep in fire, my option of a fast, handy, climb out is forfeit.

Now it gets real quiet, and the screams fade as spectators draw away for safety.

An eight-foot-wide truck puts the exit exactly eight feet away from me, straight up. My only play now is a muscle up—the gymnastic maneuver where you jump up, and using just the strength of your arms, pull the weight of your body straight up, then lock your arms.

Now, there aren't a lot of people in this world who can perform a good, fast muscle up, and I'm sure not one of them. But in June, we had to execute a hand-over-hand rope climb for our P.E. final, which I couldn't really do. But a childhood friend, Louis Mifsud, was a beast at this stuff and showed me the trick of employing a steady rhythm to maintain your momentum.

Then right there, in that instant, I have this vision of my whole life flash right before my eyes, just like they say it happens, swear to God.

It's an animated timeline suspended in the flames right in front of me, like a Super-8 film strip—long and thin, playing in fast-forward—and I recognize that I'm only a portion of the way through it, most of my life still ahead…and just a glint of something cool.

Louie's trick. *Now.* I spring up to daylight, unsure of how well my scrawny arms would execute the muscle up, but the instant my fingertips grabbed the door jam—right there in that flaming hell—I felt Louie Mifsud's powerful biceps rocket me straight out of that eight-foot-tall truck with the ease and grace of an angel. I watch as the door jamb and flames pass a country mile below my feet in slo-mo; I stick the landing perfectly square, take one precise bounce to salvation and the whole thing blows up MacGyver-style.

Just like in the movies.

And as my toes touch the ground, before my perfect bounce to redemption, before I extinguish the flames on my clothes, I say to myself: *I'm going to California.*

And so I did. And a few years later, compensation for my near-incineration by that drunk trucker would enable me to create something really bitchin' with my future California neighbor, Jack Graham.

Now the story of Jack's arrival to the Golden State is *really* nuts...

Jack Graham at Carlsbad
Skatepark, mid-construction.
John O'Malley Archive.

MR. WIZARD

Now, I don't propose that there are closer shaves than the one that I'd just had; however, let's raise the stakes to three souls and change the circumstances entirely.

At approximately the same time as my trial by fire, best calculations put the Graham family—Jack, wife Sue and their young son Mark—half a world away, struggling to escape the clutches of a Colombian drug cartel.

When I say best calculations, all that I have to go by are the stories that Jack told to me, triangulated by the first day we met and the obituary I found for him from Eureka, California, putting his age at sixty-five in 1995.

Jack Lynn Graham always told me that he hailed from Ottumwa, Iowa, and that his given name was actually Jack, not derived from the typical root of John. He stood about five feet, six inches tall. As he was perpetually tanned and tawny from a life working outdoors, when someone remarked about his trim build, Jack would point to his head—where all his calories were burned.

He credited the Iowa Jaycees (Junior Chamber of Commerce) for launching his earliest career and said that he'd use those very skills throughout his life.

I'd further argue that the Jaycees also landed Jack a world-class piece of ass. Nerds? Meet America's hottest.

So, the story goes that the Miss America contestants were all staying at the same hotel where the Jaycees were having their convention. One thing led to another, and Jack wound up marrying a beauty queen from one of the adjoining states, like a Miss Missouri or a Miss South Dakota.

I have no way of knowing whether heading off to an untamed Alaska was the original newlywed plan or not, but that's where they went. But I could never picture Jack escorting his lovely Miss Nebraska or Miss Iowa north to the tundra in one of his ugly sedans, hat boxes on the roof and sweet little outfits in the trunk.

Twenty years before the Trans-Alaska Pipeline was built, Alaska was still very raw and wide open, and it probably looked to Jack that his vision and mechanical genius just might thrive there.

And he was right.

Jack Graham's first job in Alaska was working as a salvage diver. So a couple things right off the bat about that:

First, I'll bet that he did not get much scuba training in Ottumwa.

Next? Scuba diving. In Alaska. In the winter. I mean, what the fuck? Also, 1960s wetsuit technology just sucked. But as Jack told it, his Miss Kansas or Miss Minnesota wasn't having the life of a danger-diver's wife, so he wound up buying and running a marina, which he detested and subsequently handed over to her when they parted company later on.

With his marriage and the hated marina in his rear-view mirror, Jack got back into the salvage business with a vengeance. He bought two boats suitable for the enterprise: a traditional commercial salvage vessel and a decommissioned navy landing craft he christened with the devil-baiting handle of the *Grave Robber*.

Here's how the salvage business works: a large freighter is shipwrecked, usually caught by a storm and run aground. If it's transporting valuable cargo, you negotiate a price with the insurance company to retrieve the goods in safe condition. No cargo, no pay.

Winter conditions in the Arctic Ocean turn deadly fast, and in the days before dependable weather forecasting, there was little warning of the pulverizing storms that could drown a ship in short order. So there was good enough business to be had playing a game of cutthroat with the underwriters—that is, high-paying, hairball, life-or-death business.

Notable among Jack's wagers turned deadly was a job removing a bunch of shipping containers of fresh king crab meat off the deck of a wrecked freighter.

Jack said that it was a pretty straightforward operation. The ship had been driven sideways onto the rocks in front of a cliff, and the plan was to just pop the containers onto the *Grave Robber*, deliver them to port and get paid, but a bad storm blew up fast and forced the crew to ride out the storm aboard the wreck. Sixty-mile-per-hour winds and giant waves pounded the hull. As night wore on, the storm drove the boat over the rocks and against the cliff. Next, the fuel tanks breached and spread thousands of gallons of diesel into the ocean. Every time one of those massive waves struck the hull, it rained down a disgusting mix of slippery diesel fuel and freezing sea water onto the deck.

Then things got really bad.

As wave action shoved the ship across the rocks, it began to break in half. A one-foot-wide gap opened across the deck, signaling the ship's imminent halving and collapse into the fury. Time was up.

Grasping at straws, Jack scrambled below deck and found an old box of turnbuckles. Next, the crew unspooled all the steel cable from one of the boat's cranes and ran dozens of lengths of it fore and aft across the slimy deck, splicing a turnbuckle into each length. By working feverishly all night, tightening the turnbuckles by hand, the men were able to lash that boat back together so tight that by morning the one-foot gap was close to touching.

Once the storm passed, Jack powered the ship's other crane with a jury-rigged forklift contraption and used it to offload the containers, get them to port and get paid.

Ok, so maybe Jack's Miss Oklahoma or Miss Wyoming was right—the salvage game was waaay too stressful—or maybe it was the allure of a more dependable cash stream, but Jack eventually liquidated the salvage business and started fishing for king crab.

When a job known as the *Deadliest Catch* is safer than the salvage game, that's about all you need to know. Years later, Jack would say, that of the thirty-five captains in the king crab fleet in his harbor in Alaska, he was one of only three still alive.

Jack was always creating stuff, and during his stay in Alaska, he cooked up some great inventions. I don't know where they actually fit into his timeline, but here's a couple of them:

In the old-school, "frogman" days of scuba diving, a diver's oxygen tanks were secured about the body with straps, and the whole thing was buckled together between the legs. This made it hard to ditch your gear in an emergency, and divers were dying underwater on account of it.

Jack came up with a prototype for a little quick-release clip that worked like a charm.

JACQUES? MEET JACK

Taking advantage of a visit to port by the world-renowned oceanographic research vessel *Calypso*, Jack went over and paid a visit to its captain, Jacques Cousteau, to show him his new quick-release invention.

Captain Cousteau loved Jack's little lifesaver but sadly informed Jack that the members of the *Calypso* crew were switching to backpacks later that year, and he expected the rest of the industry to follow suit, making Jack's nifty little gizmo obsolete.

THE MONEY MACHINE

Then there was what Jack called his money machine: a better razor clam dredge. Due to the razor clam's soft shell, the typical loss rate for dredging razor clams was about 90 percent, as their soft shells were crushed by the lip of the dredge as they were harvested.

Jack's innovation was to place a hose out in front of the dredge, pointing back toward the bucket and down to the sea floor. It blew a jet of water into the silt so the clams just floated up and landed gently in the bucket.

The kill rate was reduced to about 5 or 10 percent, and he brought razor clams to market in unprecedented numbers. The next year, however, the State of Alaska outlawed razor clam dredging, and the spigot to his money machine was lawyered shut.

But Jack's king crab business went great guns, and the time came to trade up to a bigger boat. The best market for such ships is in Miami, Florida, so Jack sold his boat, put his wife and son in the car and drove from Alaska to Miami. He bought a new boat and outfitted it with everything that he needed to fish for king crab the following season.

Since there was time to kill before the crab season started in Alaska and Caribbean lobsters were in season, Jack decided he'd go fish for lobster off the coast of Colombia. Now Jack was nobody's fool, so I don't understand why he didn't give the Colombian ports wide berth in the early 1970s, but he didn't, and the Graham family unwittingly pulled into port in Barranquilla on Colombia's Caribbean coast. Once docked, they offloaded their gear into dry storage and Jack set out to get the lay of the land.

They didn't have to wait long for unwanted opportunity to come knocking.

Friendly representatives of the regional drug cartel stopped by one day with glad tidings and the offer of work delivering cargo for them in the evenings.

Jack never asked what the cargo was, but he put two and two together, politely declined and decided to beat a hasty retreat out of Colombia. 2+2=gethefuckoutnow.

But the gas dock refused to sell him fuel, and all the gear he had in storage, worth about $100,000, was inaccessible.

Foremost in Jack and Sue's minds was the fragile health of their young son Mark, to whom even a minor injury could be fatal. With hopes of bribing his way out, Jack tried in vain to have money wired from his bank in Alaska, but his cables for help never left the country. Isolated, broke, out of fuel and food, the Grahams found themselves trapped in an evil, 1970s *Pirates of the Caribbean* ordeal.

Dark forces were pressing, starving them down.

Then one day, an American yacht steamed into port. Under cover of darkness, Jack rowed out to it and told the owner his story. The yacht took on a full load of fuel and offloaded it into the Graham family tanks.

They ran right through the Panama Canal, up the Pacific coast and directly into the sweet bosom of Southern California.

But the Colombians would be recouping the loss of the Graham family boat in a few short years when a major portion of the players in the skateboard industry that Jack would help to foster would be gleefully buying their product in tonnage.

I'm not sure why Jack didn't head straight home to Alaska and chose to stay in San Diego instead. He said that he'd arrived there with just the change in his pockets. It might have been the loss and trauma of the Colombian ordeal, but it could well have been San Diego's terrific weather.

Iowa and Alaska, no doubt, treated Jack to some of the worst weather that the Northern Hemisphere has to offer, and he could just have decided to chuck it.

Or Jack could have gotten off the boat, took stock of the burgeoning city of San Diego, saw that it was still plenty raw and wide open and that his clear vision and inventive, mechanical genius might just thrive there.

And of course, he was right again.

Construction was booming all over San Diego, and with Jack's affinity for large machinery, the job of grading contractor was within easy reach, so he sold his brand-new boat, purchased a brand-new bulldozer and taught himself how to be a crack operator.

Jack learned about soil compaction and composition, and just like that, he went from hauling crabs out of the Arctic Sea to slicing open the rock-hard clay of Southern California.

The Grahams took a liking to Leucadia, in San Diego's North County, with its eucalyptus trees, avocado groves and country vibe, so Jack moved his young family and tractor to the house on the corner of Vulcan Avenue and Jason Street.

The Grahams outgrew that little house in a couple years and moved directly next door, creating the vacancy that my group of expat New Yorkers would fill.

We all became immediate fans of Jack and renamed him Mr. Wizard.

But even better than having Jack's mechanical genius guiding the maintenance of our fleet of spiffy old trucks were his hair-raising stories that had us riveted in the evenings.

We'd find some next-door neighborly excuse to stop by when we spotted him working in his dirt-floor office out back after dinner. The office was jam-packed with these treasures that he'd salvaged off the bridges of shipwrecks—marvelous things all made of brass and glass and hardwood.

Jack was a great storyteller and would never foist one on you, like I'm doing here, but you'd inevitably provoke one by asking, "Mr. Graham, what is *this* thing?"

His eyes would light up, and he would tuck his cigarette into his mouth, gently pull the device off the shelf and say, "This boys, is the story of a shipwreck…"

And you were off to a storm in the Aleutians.

OPPOSITE A cool kickturn off the top by surfer/skater Kim Cespedes. © *Lance Smith/ Tracker Archive.*

ENCINITAS, CALIFORNIA

Hippie Skunkworks
House of Bahne
Bug to Butterfly in Forty-Eight Hours
The Cadillac Kid

The Skunkworks front and center.
The Tracker Trucks company cleans
up nice for the company photo. But
don't let the dog, long hair and flannel
shirts fool you, parked out back are a
Ferrari, a Lamborghini and a Pantera.
© *Tracker Archive.*

HIPPIE SKUNKWORKS

There's a popular caricature of Encinitas as this sleepy little hippie/ surf town with a pothead pathos. This is only partially true; it actually has an abundance of what any serious-minded surfer or gravity sports technologist needed: Terrific year-round surf for starters, consisting of sand bars and a dozen shelf reefs. Of the reefs, there's four beauties right in a row: Table Tops, Seaside, Cardiff and finally Swamis.

Swamis is a world-class right-hand point break and one of the jewels of the California coast; it's triply blessed by the presence of a Hindu temple atop the bluff overlooking the break. Built in 1943, the temple belongs to the Self Realization Fellowship (SRF)—hence the name Swamis.

Swamis is a lotus-eating contrast to the decaying POP Pier in Venice Beach, the surf spot central to Dogtown mythos smitten by urban blight. We're surfing a world-class right-hand point break with a hermitage of monks chanting *om* on the cliff, while the burned-out POP Pier is host to junkies, drunks, derelicts and seedy cruising for sex.

Add it up: uncrowded reef breaks, millions in skate industry money pouring into town and enough blessed hippie chicks to go around. We're all good here in Woodstock-by-the-Sea.

Thank you *very* much.

Also in abundance: superb surfboard shapers like Donald Takayama, Mike Slingerland and John Keyes, in a quantity far outstripping the needs of the local population, plus the stable of ace board builders at the Chanin and Bahne factories creating magnificent boards, polished to perfection and rendered in pastel resin tints—or, preferably, airbrushed with a trippy astral projection tableau by artist John Brieden.

Now toss in homegrown chemists from the glassing shops—all brilliant in the niche of resins and polymers—and several successful startup surf brands, like Wax Research and Fins Unlimited, and you've got a collective group of craftsmen on hand who are well equipped to innovate quickly and enthusiastically on behalf of fun.

Tom Morey designed his democratizing surf craft, the Morey Boogie board, in an Encinitas garage around this same time.

So it came to pass that as Frank Nasworthy and the Bahne Company began to have powerful success bringing Cadillac Wheels and Bahne Skateboards to the broader universe, a Hippie Skunkworks emerged out of the garages and shacks in sleepy little Encinitas that provided all the other innovations and support needed to make skateboards the high-performance rides that they are today—plus skateparks for them to call home and Warren Bolster to launch *SkateBoarder Magazine* and broadcast it to the rest of the world.

Indeed, the guys responsible for discovering the urethane wheel (Nasworthy), inventing the wide truck and molded plywood decks (Dominey and Balma), skateparks (Jack Graham and me) AND the visionary editor of *SkateBoarder Magazine*, Warren Bolster, all lived a bike ride from one another. Add to that the first half-pipe ever built—the Rampage ramp—plus MotoBoard, the first motorized skateboard, the expanse of empty streets in La Costa…and Bill Bahne.

(I'll apologize in advance for use of a smarmy California-ism.)

It was a *synergistic confluence* of people and events.

The birth of any of these inventions deserves review. But it was Nasworthy and Bahne who really tore open the Rift, so it's their stories that we should probably start with.

OPPOSITE, TOP Packing at Tracker Trucks, Lance Smith and Keith Hagen. © *Larry Balma/ Tracker Archive.*

OPPOSITE, BOTTOM Larry Balma (*left*) and I at the Tracker Factory. © *Tracker Archive.*

Bahne factory early days. Production at
Bahne went from one hundred boards
a year to one thousand boards a day in
just one year. *Bahne Archive*.

HOUSE OF BaHne

In the beginning there was Bahne and very little else.

Bahne was the singularity—the Revolution and the Skunkworks radiated out around him.

Now, if you're reading along and take exception to Bahne and company's significance, take your exception in hand and ask: *Were Cadillac Wheels involved?* The answer is yes.

You're welcome.

Z-Flex granddad Jeff Ho got his first set of Cadillac Wheels on a trip down to Bahne's to pick up surfboard fins. He saw the wheels sitting there in a box and asked, "What's going on with those things?"

Thanks, Bill.

Skateboard production at Bahne rocketed from one hundred boards a year to one thousand boards a day in a single year. This is Cupertino-like acceleration ten years before the word *startup* existed. And like Steve Jobs a decade later, Bahne's shop would produce inventions crucial to the modernization of surfboards, skis and skateboards—what Bill calls gravity-powered vehicles.

Find the Steve Jobs comparison excessive?

Here's a partial list of the inventions that have come out of Bahne's shop:

- Fins Unlimited, the removable surfboard fin system he patented in the 1960s and is still in wide use today
- The single ski, stepdad to the snowboard
- Fiberglass extruded skateboard decks
- Bahne Trucks
- Cadillac Wheels
- Automated surfboard shaping innovations
- Moonlights Productions: Bill's concert promotion company that brought first-tier performers to the very groovy little La Paloma Theatre. (I saw Toots and the Maytals open for Robert Palmer there.)

ABOVE La Paloma Theatre, perhaps the coolest place to see a show or movie ever. This day featuring appropriate hippie fare, *The Grateful Dead Movie. Richard Dowdy.*

Bahne had music for the Revolution. Bahne is the first place where roller skate parts were jettisoned and replaced by trucks and wheels built specifically for skateboards.

> *No one will ever again have the percentage of the market that Bahne had—at one time almost 100%.*
> *—Dave Dash, publisher,* SkateBoarder Magazine

Bahne Skateboards were ubiquitous in the day; everybody's first board was a Bahne. Skate hero Tony Hawk's first skateboard was a Bahne. My first new-generation board that I got in 1975 was a Bahne.

If you were riding in the mid-70s and did not start on a Bahne, well then, I'm sorry. They were terrific little sleds that came assembled in a cool white box—hey, downhill speed pioneer Denis Schufeldt went fifty miles per hour on one.

Bahne's top-to-bottom marketing savvy proved superbly effective:

- The peerless ads and posters by Jim Evans for Cadillac Wheels. Evans's illustrations exemplified the fantasy-utopian surf motif of the 1970s. Jim's Cadillac wheel ads solidified Bahne's brands and thereby the entire sport as culture-cool.
- Bahne Skateboards and Team Bahne's slick Euro-influenced styling was cribbed from Bill's foray into the ski business.
- Sponsorship of lifestyle skaters: Gregg Weaver, the beautiful, style-for-miles, transcendent Cadillac Kid, and Denis Schufeldt, yoga instructor/speed demon/spokesman/statesman, both revered for their style and skill rather than contest ranking.
- Massive financial support to *SkateBoarder Magazine*. Word was that Bahne's commitment to huge page purchases for his Bahne/Cadillac ads was enough for Surfer Publications to roll out *SkateBoarder Magazine*.

> *It wasn't advertising, I was building a sport.*
> *—BB*

Bill cultivated a brilliant skate team coached by Paul St. Pierre. St. Pierre had an uncanny eye for recruiting talent he'd forge into champions. Later on, Team Bahne become the farm league for other brands, which would buy star members away for instant credibility.

And all of this dovetailed perfectly with *SkateBoarder Magazine*'s surf-centric vision for the sport. Bahne/Cadillac blew up digital-fast in an analog age.

About the company's eventual loss of market share, Bahne is circumspect: "We couldn't meet the demand, and we sucked in a lot of competition."

But he also sucked a lot of creativity around him and nurtured it.

Here's Bill's remarks about the Skunkworks, which was referred to loosely as the "North County Skateboard Conspiracy":

> *You need creative people around you....It's a way of life, this surfing, skiing, and skateboard manufacturing. I like the friends I've acquired...We've got a fun little industry. [We] enjoy it and people enjoy the products. We drive each other to higher plateaus, but we do it with no super-economic motive. You're dealing with young people who are doing everything themselves.*

The Skunkworks was a group of extraordinary and tangent folks that came to build the infrastructure that pushed the fad to sport.

There was a platoon of people working around town at the time. Bahne noted these as cutting edge: Dominey and Balma of Tracker Trucks; Brian Logan of Logan Earth Ski; Bobby Turner, whose Turner SummerSki revolutionized slalom racing; *SkateBoarder Magazine*'s editor/photographer Warren Bolster; skatepark savant Jack Graham; and collective catalyst Di Dootson.

But I'd also add to Bill's list surfer/skater/photographer/writer Lance Smith; Mike Williams, who developed the Gullwing truck; and Henry Hester, the formidable La Costa slalom racer who created the first-ever pool riding contests, the Hester Series.

If asked, Henry would deny any Skunkworks affiliation: *You guys had your own little cabal going on up there. I was happy to come up and skate then just go home.* Yeah, well, H might have gone home to La Jolla after work, but he still had his super-sized juju bubbling in the Skunkworks stew.

OPPOSITE   The face that launched a million crushes, Ellen O'Neal. *Jim Goodrich.*

Bahne/Cadillac contest. *Bahne Archive.*

BUG TO BUTTERFLY IN
FORTY-EIGHT HOURS

On April 26 and 27, 1975, Bahne and company produced Ocean Festival, a two-day gravity sport fusion/extravaganza held at the Del Mar Fairgrounds. It featured dozens of exhibits and demonstrations on surfing, skiing, scuba diving, hang gliding, rock climbing, skydiving, dune buggy and catamaran riding.

Saturday night ended with an epic midnight concert by Honk, the marquee surf band of the day. Sunday night's closing feature was Philippe Cousteau, author, cinematographer and film director for the research vessel *Calypso*.

All of this, decades before the Be-Ins and Burning Men of the next century. Oceanfest would finally squeeze the thing from fad to sport.

It also featured a skateboard contest, the Bahne/Cadillac championships, but the fairgrounds are flat, so for starters, they had to construct a huge ramp.

> *We wanted a contest and didn't have a hill so we built one.*
> —BB

> *No one realizes what Bahne did for skateboarding alone for three years, toting those ramps around and promoting contests. He's the most under-publicised promoter of the sport.*
> —Frank Nasworthy

Although there were other significant contests of the day, it was this one that actually codified the thing.

Why?

The perfect timing of it for one, April 1975; the sterling Bahne/Cadillac imprimatur for another; and because the congregation of competitors that emerged that day become the very best skaters of the seventies: Peggy Oki, the Logan family, Ty Page, Jay Adams, Tony Alva, Skitch Hitchcock and Chris Yandall among them.

Additionally, to avoid any appearance of bias, Bahne did not allow his own team to compete. That means no Ellen Berryman, undefeated women's freestyle champion, and no men's world freestyle champ Bob Mohr. Team Bahne slalom specialist Paul Eng entered as an independent and took first place. Soul stylist Gregg Weaver was a judge.

Bill recusing his superlative team like that was essentially leaving a handful of trophies on the table, and yet there's no shortage of aging hot shots and ephemera, a few rightly, still dining out on that day.

You're welcome.

Why did Bahne put himself through it all?

Because we had to have it, and if I didn't do it, nobody else was going to.

And to thems who stand on their chairs and over-claim about that day I would say: *Dude, you're blocking our view of Honk and Philippe Cousteau. You've dissed Bahne's hospitality AND you're riding Bill's wheels. Sit the fuck down.*

Bill Bahne kept his own best interest in a blind trust while he midwifed the birth of a sport.

> *If it weren't for Bahne we wouldn't have a skateboard industry.*
> —Ron Bennett, Bennett Trucks

I was out drinking with a successful young skatepark developer and turned to him and said: *Hey, you like your groovy job in skate? You can thank Bill Bahne for that.*

You're welcome.

OPPOSITE, TOP   Skitch Hitchcock handstand using his homemade hand skates. Skitch had numerous marvelous inventions like these. *Warren Bolster.*

OPPOSITE, BOTTOM   Ocean Festival poster. *Bahne Archive.*

Gregg Weaver soul arch, Black Hill,
early days. *Warren Bolster.*

THE CADILLAC KID

First off, go to YouTube and watch the 1975 film clip of fourteen-year-old Gregg Weaver skating the Black Hill. Go do a search for "Gregg Weaver"—it'll be the first clip that pops up.

In truth, this should always come first because it gets right to the original thought of Skate better than anything else.

Seriously, go to YouTube right now and watch it.

Take your time, this will keep.

The clip is a three-minute, slo-mo study that showcases the subtleties of Weaver's style-for-miles skating. It speaks in a surf-centric vocabulary and is polar opposite to the piles of jarring hard-rock clips that have all but obliterated the memory of this era.

A masterful little piece of cinematography, it's shot in one long, focus-pulled close-up by cameraman Spider Wills. Gregg traverses the hill in luxurious slow-motion on one of his own hand-carved longboards.

Spider is a master of the art of following a moving target with a motion picture camera and keeping it in focus (pulling focus). His sequence of Gregg soul-styling down the Black Hill at La Costa is one of the most poetic pieces of film shot on any sport, however pixelated, and a sublime style throw-down. It showcases longboard skating decades before it became popular and epitomizes a stylistic essence that is still pervasive today in north San Diego County.

Gregg Weaver was a quiet kid with natural grace and style. Dubbed "The Cadillac Kid," he became the icon of fluidity and fun in 1975 when he appeared as the original poster boy for the sport.

How'd he land the job?

Frank Nasworthy needed a skater to photograph for the inaugural series of ads that Cadillac Wheels was running in *Surfer Magazine*. (*SkateBoarder Magazine* was still a year away.) He'd made plans to shoot with a different guy who blew him off when the surf came up.

Stood up and bummed out, Nasworthy was standing in the street at Stone Steps beach when fourteen-year-old Gregg skated by. He impressed both Frank and sharp-eyed surf photographer Art Brewer.

They flagged Gregg down and asked him to model for the ad.

Brewer's photos caught Gregg's smooth surf style and good looks. The resulting advertisements elevated skate to parity with surfing.

Weaver invented the boardslide—this is a maneuver, where instead of your typical 180-degree kickturn at the top of a bowl, Gregg chucked coveted traction and redirected the board to slide sideways along the rim. I watched him perfect it at our skatepark over the course of about a week.

The boardslide is a sublime and magical move, hard to do and fun to watch. Stalwart eighties skater Steve Caballero's boardslides are probably my favorite.

The last thing that Gregg with two gs did really well is skate through his growth spurt. The transition from mosquito-weight to man-sized will kill a skating career, but Gregg just expanded and became more explosive.

You can still see his classic flow style imprinted on the North County community. I was watching a recent clip of a guy surfing with inordinate beauty and style. You could see it from a mile away: *This guy's from North County*. He was from Cardiff.

I really can't say if Gregg is the chicken or the egg here, but his influence clearly remains today.

OPPOSITE Gregg Weaver lip slide, Carlsbad Skatepark. *Warren Bolster.*

Black Hill's earliest days. All the boards handmade, Chicago roller skate trucks.
© *Tracker Archive*.

LA COSTA

Family Style
The Fastest Man Alive
Four Years of Halcyon Days
Betsy Ross-y Stuff Aside
Renaissance Fair of Fast

Kids' contest. © *Lance Smith/ Tracker Archive.*

FAMILY STYLE

In 1975, La Costa was already a world-renowned destination as a luxury spa and golf resort. Built and run by mob money, it's financing by the Central States Teamsters was orchestrated by Mafia don Moe Dalitz.

Moe was one of the twentieth century's most notorious gangsters and, according to the FBI, "the individual who oversees the operations of the Cosa Nostra families in Las Vegas."

So it should have been a surprise to no one that La Costa was a notorious mob hangout.

After the resort was established, Moe planned to build a whole zip code's worth of exclusive homes intertwined with its golf courses spreading back up the mountain behind the resort, where there's a triple-whammy view of the Batiquitos Lagoon, the Pacific Ocean and the setting sun. Bam Bam Bam. What could go wrong?

What went wrong was the recession of the 1970s.

Unfortunately, right after all the streets and sidewalks were installed, the recession put the kibosh on any further development. This no doubt pissed off the gangsters, but there was nothing that anyone could do about it, and the mob found themselves the proud owners of a square mile of vacant hills paved with brand-new roads and sidewalks, no traffic and no police whatsoever.

God is indeed great.

La Costa is a suburb of Encinitas, where the Bahne factory was pouring Cadillac Wheels onto the streets. Local surfers took quick note of the mob's free skate zone, and La Costa became the place to go and skate when the surf was flat.

They first gravitated to El Fuerte Street, a major artery of the development, which came to be called the Black Hill. The Black Hill runs clockwise down the spine of the mountain on a steep grade. It's extra wide, ending in a nice, soft uphill runout.

With its fresh blacktop, desert scrub and California sunsets, it provided a stark, cinematic backdrop that accentuated the subject and provided the canvas that Warren Bolster used to create his original iconic images, those that would herald the Revolution—images powerful enough to convince *Surfer Magazine* to start up *SkateBoarder Magazine* and put Bolster in charge.

And it was there on the Black Hill that a switch was flipped, and it went from being a place to go when the surf was flat to a place for skateboarders.

A place to call home.

A place to skate.

Click. You're a sport.

Approaching La Costa was like watching a ski resort in negative, with skaters carving down fresh black asphalt instead of snow. During the week, speed freak John Hughes and company would be drag racing, solo and in packs.

On Sundays, there'd be slalom racing, with prize money staked by entree fees. Winner takes all.

The mobsters weren't real thrilled about inadvertently opening a ten-thousand-acre free skate zone but looked the other way until things got too crazy, with packs of guys racing downhill and getting towed back up by car pretty much all the time.

Eventually, Mo sent representatives, who turned out to be pretty cool about it. They advised that the scene be moved to a less conspicuous location. Seeing as we'd spent five years skating on the mob's dime, I'd say they were damned-skippy cool about it.

The next spot was Venado Street on the farthest edge of the development—much more discreet. It's adjacent to a California arroyo where the San Marcos Creek runs year-round into the Batiquitos Lagoon. There is a waterfall and pool there, and it is known as Box Canyon.

It's at Box Canyon that the Sunday races flourished, professional skateboarding began and the nascent industry emerged.

In an icon-driven market, the game is to have the best guys ride for you, do rad shit and get their picture in *SkateBoarder Magazine*. And it's the same today, except there's much more media and the pay's way better.

With few exceptions, this meant working with either LA-based adjunct writer/photographer Craig Stecyk or Warren Bolster, editor and primary photographer of *SkateBoarder Magazine*, but mainly Warren. And if you wanted to shoot with Warren, you came to La Costa, because that's where Warren lived.

And you definitely came on Sunday.

A family of curves or surfaces at a constant angle.

Racing requires community. You come together to compete, to measure one another and to wager. You need enough people to make the prize money interesting and some to run it. You do this every week for a bunch of years, and it gets to be family.

The Sunday races were served family style to a unique cast of characters.

When I say family style, I mean that families came, such as the Turner family: Bobby Turner, wife Peggy, brother Vince and his incredible team, including Michael Williams, wife Rebecca and their twins—plus top riders like Steve Schisler, Tommy Ryan and rock star skater/ski racer Bobby Piercy. Bobby Turner was clearly the elder statesman on the hill, he had a singular alpine vision of skateboard design and racing. Ski construction, ski racing, please.

The Balmas came and held down for Tracker Trucks: Larry, wife Mary and daughter Laurie, along with other family, friends and Tracker team members. Always a strong competitor, you'd count photographer Lance Smith among these. Partner Dave Dominy, his sister Dawn and race director Di Dootson also sat with Tracker.

Gordon & Smith (G&S) team members Henry Hester and Bob Skoldberg were like brothers-in-law, with H dating Bobby's sister. Both were always there to win.

Good racers too young to drive came with enthusiastic family in tow; Peter Tholl came with his dad and sister Sue. And before he morphed into the renowned surf photographer "T-Sherm," Steve Sherman was a terrific slalom racer. Steve came chauffeured by his father, scientist Brig Sherman.

Brig would go a long way to classing up our act.

You'd count on seeing the Berryman sisters: Ellen and her chaperone/sister/muse Cindy. Ellen and Cindy were both lovely, sprout-fed Encinitas girls, and you would not miss them on the hill.

The Rhino Racing team was a pair of guys who specialized in the all-but-abandoned practice of catamaran riding and always represented with their girlfriends and the other members of their terrific cover band Bratz. No day jobs here. Skate all day and rock all night. A version of that band is still playing today, in versions of the same bars.

Unsurprisingly, intradisciplinary love affairs sprouted among peers, like racers Kim Cespedes and Tommy Ryan and freestyle pros Ellen O'Neal and Ed Nadalin.

Warren Bolster actually lived nearby in La Costa with his lovely wife, Suzy—you don't get more family than that.

However, with roots deep into the 1960s, it was the Logan family that really brought dynastic cred to the whole scene. Siblings Brian, Bruce, Brad and Robin were all winning competitors, and Brian Logan built the family Logan Earth Ski brand and team into one of the most prestigious of the 1970s. Brian remains one of the pillars of skate. Mix team riders Laura

ABOVE Turner SummerSki style. Ski materials, ski style please. © *Tracker Archive.*

OPPOSITE Dave Dominey running cones. Dave's inventions have had a profound effect on gravity sports. Most trucks now are basically built like Tracker Trucks, and his Streamline brand of urethane universal joints used for boat masts helped change sailboat racing forever. © *Tracker Archive.*

Thornhill, Torger Johnson, Jay Adams and Tony Alva into the clan and you've got an extremely formidable crew.

But it was their mother, Barbara Logan, who was the heartbeat of the hill. Barbara embodied family love up there. She was quick to adopt worthy strays—Tony Alva lived at her house for a while. Laura Thornhill and Robin were like sisters.

Barbara Logan is deeply missed since her passing in 2007.

The families and strays disassembled into five clans:

The Logan family
Team Bahne
The Tracker team
The Turner team
The Gordon & Smith team

The Five Families of La Costa—six if you count the mob.

OPPOSITE The beautiful and stylish Ellen O'Neal skating at La Costa. *Warren Bolster.*

Denis Shufeldt, La Costa speed run. Note, early arms-out wind fairing technique was thought to be advantageous. Arms tucked back was later found to be faster. *Warren Bolster.*

THE FASTEST MAN ALIVE

Denis Schufeldt came from a section of San Diego that's known as Birdland; it's a dagger-shaped burg formed by the intersection of Route 163 on the east and the 805 Freeway on the west, where all the streets have avian names. Birdland was the golden triangle of the primordial San Diego skate soup.

There was a guy named Paul St. Pierre who lived in Birdland who was the core of the thing and he would become the coach of Team Bahne.

If Paul had very high standards, it's understandable. Here are some of the other guys who came out of Paul's Birdland: elite racers Bobby Piercy, Steve Schisler, Pat Flanagan and Conrad Mioshi; freestyle/pool pros Dennis Martinez and Doug "Pineapple" Saladino and Denis Schufeldt—that's a cohort you wouldn't like to compete against.

Something of a Bobby Knight–type, St. Pierre was known for being a very hard marker and plenty tough on the riders, but on St. Pierre's watch, Team Bahne would produce the bulk of the original first-string San Diego pro skaters, including world freestyle champions Bob Mohr and Ellen Berryman. And he groomed Martinez and Saladino, only to have them stolen away by competing teams.

Denis Schufeldt, however, was an entirely different kind of deal. Schufeldt was the first guy to take up downhill speed racing as a serious pursuit.

A longtime yoga instructor, Denis used his impeccable balance and core training to hold the perfect isometric poses needed to control those original unstable little skateboards and go fifty miles per hour on one.

Yeah, I know, plenty of people bombed hills back then—usually to their regret—but Denis took a methodic scientific approach. He had nerves of steel and inimitable style. He would carve bold turns at speed, arms thrown back, knees forward—never a thought to falling.

Already a wise and transcendent man in his twenties, Schufeldt channeled the Rift straight outta Bahne and right up to the Black Hill. From Bahne to Bolster. Then snap! From Bolster to the world.

Paste your *Right Stuff* comparisons here.

Plus, Denis-with-one-N was a real class act. Handsome, eloquent and even-tempered, he parlayed his reputation as Fastest Man Alive into his greatest role: sage and spokesman for the sport. For years, Denis was the go-to guy for interviews, color commentary and host for television broadcasts.

When the Mattel Corporation entered the skateboard market in a big way with its Magnum Skateboard line, it built the brand around Denis, and he was the perfect spokesman.

Schufeldt was never imitated.

Crib his style? Mmmm…

Fake the substance? Naaa.

My personal favorite Schufeldt-ism was to broadcaster Bud Palmer after watching Henry Hester go down hard during the final race at the Hang Ten World Championships in 1976 (**BOOF!**).

The pavement never forgets, Bud.

OPPOSITE Racer riding the distinctive Mattel Magnum trucks at a race in Akron, Ohio. *John O'Malley Archive.*

Box Canyon giant slalom overview with
Tommy Ryan mid-course. The urethane
contrails left around the cones suggest
a summer day, well into the race.
Di Dootson Archive.

FOUR YEARS
OF HALCYON DAYS

Each clan had its own camp of cars and crew, each betting on their own equipment and technique.

The Logan team rode muscle-car wood decks fast and hard like Cobra GTs.

G&S rode flexible wood/fiberglass laminate boards called "Fiberflex." The G&S guys had factory money, with a manager, team uniforms and a strong churchgoing vibe. They were establishment, like Porsche.

The Turner team was devoted to Bobby Turner's perfect vision of ski-style slalom racing, and they were scrappy. They raced hard and raced pretty and always lobbied for tight slalom courses where their parallel ski-stance had the advantage.

They were like a dirt lot Ferrari team.

Which worked better? That depended on the day. For as futuristic as Bobby Turner's SummerSkis were, Tony Alva would come and win on a stock oak board a lot. So it really depended on the rider, the course and the day.

But never the weather, these were four years of halcyon days. With Venado Street set just behind the coastal marine layer, every Sunday was blue skies—never a cancellation for weather.

The whole Sabbath-day race ritual started out pretty ragtag, with old-school traffic cones and a timing system of flags and stopwatches; however, Brig Sherman decided pretty fast that the flags and stopwatches had to go, and he built us a portable light-beam system that measured results in thousandths.

OPPOSITE Racer Tommy Ryan being chased by Michael Williams. Sunday race warm-up. © *Lance Smith/Tracker Archive.*

ABOVE, LEFT Henry Hester, the thinking man's racer. *Warren Bolster.*

ABOVE, RIGHT Don Bostwick in the money today. © *Lance Smith/Tracker Archive.*

RIGHT Lance Smith race day. © *Larry Balma/Tracker Archive.*

Things fell into place nicely, and soon race director Di Dootson was herding them cats through Brig Sherman's timing system fast and frosty. And out of these hot-and-cold rivalries came community and innovation.

SANTA CRUZ

In truth, not every invention came out of SoCal. The guys from Santa Cruz Skateboards, Jay Shuirman and Rich Novack, were outlier innovators who came up with key skate part inventions, like the first sealed-bearing wheels—Road Riders—and use of graphite composites for slalom boards. Their distance from the insular SoCal mindset gave the partners an empirical view of the sport, and they thrived in their parallel universe.

Santa Cruz Skateboards had a great team that Jay and Rich would bring down to race. Most notable among their team riders was John Hutson. John was an impeccable racer and a full-time cross-training athlete, guaranteed to win more than his share of contests.

Rich Novak would go on to grow Santa Cruz into the largest brand of skate-related stuff in the world today, despite the untimely death of Jay Shuirman in 1979 at age forty.

Now Jay Shuirman was something very special.

Brilliant and powerful, I always felt that Jay's connection to the god source—whatever one calls that—was fast and wide. When you met Jay, you got the vague impression that it would be very foolish to fuck with Jay, that *that* would be a really, really bad idea. NorCal filmmaker John Malvino was in the room when Jay jumped up and kicked the ceiling in a random display of explosive power. I think that you walk this world a lot of lifetimes before meeting a soul like Jay Shuirman.

What do four years of sublime Sundays add up to?

Hey, the weekly races were very, very, big fun, but the whole thing was much deeper than that. I overheard someone say, "We didn't just talk about community. We were community."

OPPOSITE Henry Hester (*left*), Bob Skoldberg (*center*) and Bobby Piercy. If you came to win, your payday is the other side of these guys and good luck with that. © *Lance Smith/ Tracker Archive.*

A very cheery Di Dootson.
© Lance Smith/Tracker Archive.

BETSY ROSS-Y STUFF ASIDE

Why did Di Dootson start coming to La Costa?

She certainly liked to ride and would cruise the hill "slow and show."

Di's got a taste for racing; she'd made the yearly trek to watch the Baja 500 in its early days.

While not a blood relative of Tracker Trucks co-founder Dave Dominey, they are certainly cousins-by-cause.

Di and Dave grew up together as navy brats in Hawaii, their dads a pilot and a pastor, respectively. They shared a house together in Leucadia where Dave designed the prototype for his game-changing Tracker Trucks on the kitchen table. Their garage was the first Tracker workshop.

One Sunday early on, Di showed up at the Black Hill with a clipboard and just started taking care of things. She ran the races and kept score, but more importantly, she looked ahead. She planned, advocated, budgeted and provided counseling and adult supervision. In 1976, she launched a newspaper, the *National Skateboard Review* (NSR), and published everything in there. The complete archive is available online.

Di never barked orders or picked sides. She'd listen to the squabbling, then boil it all down into rules and process. At day's end she'd read it all back: *Ok…Tommy gets the money…and so from now on it's gonna be 3/10ths of a second for hitting a cone…three cones and you scratch. And we're gonna run TWO races: one giant slalom and one tight slalom. Everybody? Right?*

Uh-huh.

Di was trained as a recreational therapist, so she is inclined to medicate with fun. But more importantly, her specialty is dysfunctional children. Okay, stop laughing.

It was the perfect skill set for managing this group of actual children, emotional children and grown-ups chasing after their childhood. She remained calm when elite racers stomped their feet, threw down their expensive slalom boards and acted like four-year-olds. She let them run their mouths and kept 'em on course.

And for years, Di stayed, running those races and printing her paper—where someone else might get bored and just want to run cones, she stayed.

Or pick out a boyfriend and split.

Or go sideways one day and tell everyone to kindly fuck right off.

With passion and purpose, Di stayed; she stayed and held us all together.

Di Dootson was the tincture in the asphalt that made it all hum.

The four drops of catalyst into a bucket of bad children to harden into a shiny new sport.

And the community loved Di right back—manufacturers ran ads in her paper, folks subscribed; Jack and I were the publishers. But the real testimony was Warren Bolster's stalwart support. There was no end to free photos and articles given on the down-low, knowing that *SkateBoarder Magazine* would frown on aiding and abetting another publication, however teeny.

She took that clipboard and sewed together a sport, one Sunday at a time.

But all this Betsy Ross-y stuff aside, Di's a real party. And Di likes buff guys with their (shirts) off. After the race course was cleaned up, certain consenting-age adults would head back to her secluded home with in-ground pool in Leucadia for debauchery-lite partying of BBQ, skinny dipping and wine coolers (hey, it was the seventies).

So, you say to me. *You've seen Di nekkid?*

Yeah, and she has a terrific rack.

She still paddles on a Hawaiian outrigger canoe team and competes wherever the game's good.

TOP, LEFT Di Dootson calling a race in Akron, Ohio. *Warren Bolster.*

TOP, RIGHT Di Dootson, slow and show, Box Canyon. © *Larry Balma/Tracker Archive.*

LEFT Di Dootson in charge. Clipboard, lawn chair, stopwatch. © *Lance Smith/Tracker Archive.*

MIDDLE, RIGHT *National Skateboard Review* office with Di Dootson and Lance Smith. *Di Dootson Archive.*

BOTTOM, RIGHT Dave Dominey surf style, Escondido Reservoir. © *Lance Smith/Tracker Archive.*

Bobby Piercy, always fast and
stylish, this day skating bare midriff.
Warren Bolster.

Renaissance Fair of Fast

Every Sunday for four years, there was guaranteed money to be made riding a skateboard at La Costa. All you had to do was come up to the Hill and beat the likes of Henry Hester or Tony Alva in a slalom race.

And good luck with that, because right behind those guys there was an easy dozen of the best racers of the last century, each with their own unbeatable days.

Every week for four years, the Sunday races brought out the best competitors from all over. And not just to run cones, downhill racers and freestyle skaters were guaranteed to show up in force too. It was like a Renaissance Fair of Fast.

The freestyle skaters who came out were an incredible sideshow; they'd arrive all revved up from team practice and buzz around the Hill busting out a truckload of new tricks while the race crews were skating, walking back up the course and tweaking their gear.

And this would be the most elite group of their day, including every current and future men's and women's freestyle champion for the next handful of years, both young and old: Ty Page, Bruce Logan, Steve Cathey, Bob Mohr, Ellen O'Neal, Dennis Martinez, Doug Saladino, 1960s champ Torger Johnson, Laura Thornhill and the incomparable Ellen Berryman among them.

Barefoot stylist Ed Nadalin drifted in after winning his amateur freestyle title. He said that La Costa energized his career, and he turned pro. This is a pretty common story. The Hill had a really positive vibe; everything that you

RACE RESULTS

February 15 - SLALOM

1st John Sigurdson	9.5
2nd Chris Smith	9.7
3rd Jeffrey Junkins	9.8

February 22 - GIANT SLALOM

Winners

1st Torger Johnson	22.6
2nd Brian Logan	22.8
3rd Glen Tucker	22.9

Other Racers

David Dominy	23.0 (F)
Pete Tholl	23.0 (F)
Steve Schisler	23.0 (F)
Brian Bracker	24.1 (F)
John Sigurdson	24.6
John O'Malley	25.2
Layne Oaks	26.2
Chris Smith	26.2
Bruce Logan	26.7
Marty Schaub	27.6
Mike Robinson	28.1
Dennis Martinez	38.0
Jeffrey Junkins	DQ
Buck Norris	DQ
Bobby Turner	DQ
Lance Smith	DQ

SLALOM

Winners

1st John Sigurdson	8.4
2nd Pete Tholl	9.3
3rd none qualified	

Other Racers

Steve Schisler	10.1 (F)
Chris Smith	DQ
Glenn Tucker	DQ
Layne Oaks	DQ
Buck Norris	DQ
David Dominy	DQ
Bobby Turner	DQ

February 29 - HEAD-TO-HEAD SLALOM

Winners

1st Henry Hester
2nd Pete Tholl
3rd Lance Smith
4th John Sigurdson

Other Racers

Brian Craft
Marty Schaub
Wilbur Crane
Chris Smith
Mike Williams
Jeffrey Junkins
Steve Lis
John Slavin
Dave Smith
Dennis Martinez
Brian Logan
Steve Schisler

GIANT SLALOM

Winners

1st Tony Alva	21.0
2nd Henry Hester	21.2
3rd Bob Skoldberg	21.1

Other Racers

Jim Muir	21.6 (F)
Chris Smith	22.8 (F)
Brian Bracken	22.9 (F)
Mike Williams	21.8 (F)
Brian Logan	22.9
Lance Smith	23.0
John Sigurdson	23.9
Dennis Martinez	24.0
Steve Lis	24.5
Dodie Hackenmack	25.3
Buck Norris	25.6
Marty Schaub	25.9
Bobby Garcia	28.7
Wilbur Crane	31.6
Robin Van Essen	42.1

March 7 - GIANT SLALOM

Winners

1st Tony Alva	24.3
2nd Chris Yandall	24.7
3rd Jim Muir	24.6

Other Racers

Brian Logan	24.5 (F)
Lance Smith	26.0 (F)
Cliff Coleman	26.2 (F)
Jim O'Mahoney	26.5
Brian Bracken	26.7
Dennis Martinez	26.9
Pete Tholl	27.1
Ted Sommer	27.3
David Fisher	27.6
Marty Schaub	27.7
Paco Prieto	27.9
Mike Robinson	27.9
Dodie Hackenmack	28.4
Tim Moir	28.5
Chris Fisher	28.7
Vince Andrade	29.1
Latosse Hartwell	30.1
Jeff Sand	30.6
Warren Bolster	DQ

March 14 - GIANT SLALOM

Winners

1st Henry Hester	25.0
2nd Bob Skoldberg	25.0
3rd Tom Sims	25.9

Other Racers

Dennis Martinez	26.6 (F)
Layne Oaks	27.1 (F)
Mike Robinson	27.7 (F)
Eddie Katz	28.2
Joe Roper	28.6
Gary Kating	29.0
Bruce Logan	29.4
Marty Schaub	29.5

Vince Andrade	2?
Tim Moir	2?
Brad Logan	29.?
Steven Whitehead	30.?
Rory Russell	31.3
Paul Copesky	31.9
Laura Thornhill	35.9
Jeffrey Junkins	DQ
Curt Lindgren	DQ

March 21 - GIANT SLALOM

Winners

1st Henry Hester
2nd Jim Muir
3rd Chris Yandall

Other Racers

Desiree Crisp
Rebecca Williams
John O'Malley
Marty Schaub
Layne Oaks
Joe Lynch
Lance Smith
Randy Clark
Brett Reynolds
Dwight Williams
Gary North
Curtis Hesselgarve

March 28 - GIANT SLALOM

Winners

1st Bob Skoldberg	21.1
2nd Henry Hester	21.7
3rd Tony Alva	22.0

Other Racers

Mike Williams	22.0 (F)
Tommy Ryan	22.3 (F)
John Krisik	22.7 (F)
Lance Smith	23.4
Bruce Logan	23.5
Jamie Hart	24.0
David Dominy	24.6
Joe Lynch	24.5
Gary Hoverg	24.6
Steve Lis	24.7
Vince Turner	25.5
Chris Smith	27.4
John Sigurdson	DQ

SLALOM

Winners

1st Lance Smith	8.4
2nd John Krisik	8.5
3rd Steve Lis	8.6

Other Racers

Pete Tholl	8.3 (F)
Steve Schisler	8.6 (F)
Buck Norris	8.9 (F)
Jamie Hart	
Vince Turner	11.5
Scott Swanson	11.8
Don Becker	DQ
John Jain	DQ
Mike Williams	

ABOVE Race results for February 15—March 28, year? Not sure. *Di Dootson Archive.*

OPPOSITE, TOP Influential surfboard shaper, inventor of the fish-type surfboard, Steve Lis running cones. © *Lance Smith/Tracker Archive.*

OPPOSITE, BOTTOM The fast and stylish racer Conrad Mioshi. © *Lance Smith/Tracker Archive.*

brought was welcome—freestyle, pool riding, new inventions—and it was all about nurturing the new.

All the while, *SkateBoarder Magazine* photographer/editor Warren Bolster would be roaming the Hill recording all of it: the racing, the freestyle ballet and whatever random weirdness popped up. When Warren saw someone he wanted to feature in the magazine, he'd schedule a one-on-one photo shoot for a weekday.

Warren also cultivated creative talent from the Hill: photographers Lance Smith and Jim Goodrich would become regular contributors to *SkateBoarder Magazine*.

He derailed Cindy Berryman from law school and onto a successful writing career. I wrote some.

I'm not sure what it's like these days, but in 1976, finding a skateboarder to put together one thousand words on deadline was a very tall order, so Warren was happy to grow the talent that he needed where he could.

He spotted fifteen-year-old Glenn E. Friedman through a mail submission and mentored him with advice and technical information in a series of handwritten letters. He tapped Aikido master and surfboard fin-foil Curtis Hesselgrave for a monthly Skate Safe column in which Curtis demonstrated martial arts rolling techniques that minimize injury when falling—techniques that I sadly still rely on today.

So here is the birth of professional skateboarding, but even more importantly than the weekly stake, this is where business was done. If you wanted to skate for G&S, Bahne, Tracker, Turner, Gullwing, Logan or various wheel companies or shoot with *SkateBoarder Magazine*—you shaped up on the Hill. If you came with a factory/deck sponsorship, you'd pick up your wheel and truck sponsor here.

Street slalom is a hybrid of ski racing and road racing, so the buzz on the Hill was much like a sport with wheels—little bivouacs of cars and guys and equipment. The racing was done either surf or ski style.

The stiffest rivalry was between the G&S and Turner SummerSki teams, with Logan team riders on oak boards winning and placing regularly, but nothing embodies the clash of forces more than the rivalry between Henry Hester and Bobby Piercy.

OPPOSITE $500? A damn good payday. In today's dollars? Just under $2,000. © *Lance Smith/Tracker Archive.*

	1	2	3	4	BEST	PLACE
David Andrews	22.983	23.551	23.225	23.230	22.983	F-2
Bob Skoldberg	22.839	23.351	DNF	22.295	22.295	F-1
Steve Sherman	23.443	24.292	24.356	23.664	23.443	6
Steve Evans	23.290	23.551	23.426	23.456	23.290	F-5
Randy Smith	24.313	24.644	23.945	DQ	23.945	10
Manny Schaub	DNF	24.421	23.920	23.927	23.920	7
Charlie Ranson	23.995	24.222	24.179	23.288	23.288	F-4
TR — Turner	23.985	24.203	24.477	24.323	23.985	11
Pat Ferguson — intrp	DQ	DQ	26.152	25.105	25.105	15
Pete Thrall — LES	24.420	24.962	DNF	PASS	24.420	12
John Hutson — Sa Cruz	23.410	23.655	23.616	23.221	23.221	F
Steve Schisler — Bruce	24.671	DQ	35.360	25.103	24.671	
Cliff Coleman — Sa Cruz	24.720	DNF	25.541	24.492	24.492	
Don Bostick — Sa Cruz	24.181	23.787	24.598	24.114	23.787	8
Torger Johnson — LES	24.214	23.959	24.450	23.810	23.810	9
Bruce Logan — LES	28.854	DNF	30.073	23.964	28.854	16
5 Steve Evans	23.660	23.177	23.821		23.177	3
4 Charlie Ranson	23.254	23.646	23.789		23.646	5
3 John Hutson	23.188	23.402	23.286		23.188	2
2 D Andrews	23.050	23.157	DQ		23.050	1
1 B Skolbe	22.803	22.952	30.813		22.803	

PRO B.S.

sec/cone /cone
#3 = DQ
#4 = DQ

1st – Bob Skoldberg $ – 500 –
2nd – David Andrews $ – 100 –
3rd – Steve Evans $ – 50 –
3rd – $ –

Piercy was a rock star/hedonist with a superiority complex above and beyond the standard-issue shoulder chip that the Turner team had.

Bobby had this extra swagger because, well, he was Piercy and you weren't. Bobby could hold his blow and make you feel like you were happy to meet him while he took your race money, went right through your stash and put the moves on your girlfriend.

Bobby was a charismatic guy, a terrific guy and a really good-looking guy. Women loved Piercy, and Bobby loved them back hard.

Henry Hester's surf style and factory affiliation put him on the opposite end of the spectrum. Just this side of being buff and a pretty boy, Henry (also H or HH) was a thinking man with his head deeply in the game. And in stark contrast to the heathen Piercy, H rode for Gordon & Smith, a loud and proud churchgoing Christian company.

Henry was a beast on a giant slalom course and nearly unbeatable.

H had a keen eye for competition and was ever vigilant for the arrive-and-slay outlier. He'd point to Z-Boy Jay Adams as the guy to beat whenever Jay showed up. Henry believed that Jay could come up and just blast through the course unaccountably and smoke everyone by a couple seconds. And although Jay never did race, H was probably right.

The assembly of passionate talent that converged every week was unparalleled. Here's a partial list of attendees, in no particular order:

Tommy Ryan, Henry Hester, Bobby Piercy, Bob Skoldberg, Steve Schisler, Chris Yandall, Lance Smith, Dale "Sausage" Smith, Danny Trailer, Neil Graham, Steve Lis, Vince Turner, Joe Roper, Ty Page, David "Pappy" Andrews, Jack Smith, Bob Bergen, Dale Dobson, Lance Smith, Dave Dominy, Tony Padilla, Steve Menas, Cindy Loyd, Bobby Fraas, Earl Smith, Charlie Ransom, Guy Grundy, Mark Matina, John Sigurdson, Brad Hurst, Chris Henderson, Eddie Katz and Vince Andrade, Tommy Ryan, Joe Roper, John Hudson, Torger Johnson, Dennis Martinez, Lane Oaks, Peter Tholl, Jeff Jenkins, Dave "Fibre Fats" McIntyre, Robyn Van Essen, Jim Muir, Michael Williams, Torger Johnson, Brian Logan, Robin Logan, Bruce Logan, Brad Logan, Barbara Logan, Tony Alva, Cliff Coleman, Don Sheridan, Sally Ann Miller, Jim O'Mahoney, Dodie Hackenmack, Warren Bolster, Tom Sims, Jamie Hart, Dave Fischer, Tom Padaka, Tim Moir, Bob Mohr, Doug "Pineapple" Saladino, Curtis Hesselgrave, Joe Lynch, Desiree Crisp, Rebecca Williams, Kim Cespedes, Steve Cathey, Laura Thornhill, Ellen O'Neal, Paul Hoffman, Jim Goodrich, Ellen Berryman, Cindy Berryman, Bob Jarvis, Conrad Mioshi, Robin Allaway, Ed Nadalin, Kathy Bromeister, Paul Eng, Paul St. Pierre, Ray Allen, Dave Carson, Randy Travis, David Hackett, Paul Hackett, Skitch Hitchcock, Garrison, Denis Schufeldt, Russ Gosnell, Ray Allen, Mike Weed, Russ Howell, Paul Hoffman, Steve Olson, Joe Roper, John Yaz, Gary Keating, Steve Lis, John Krisic, Rory Russell, Jay Shuirman, Rich Novak, Judith Cohen, John Hughes, Don Bostick

Apologies to any regulars and regular spectators I've omitted

OPPOSITE Henry Hester leaving the starting block with (*left to right*) Bobby Piercy, Mike Williams and Steve Schisler paying close attention. *Warren Bolster.*

For fans of women skaters, Sundays on the Hill was the greatest show on earth. Laura Thornhill, Robin Logan, Ellen O'Neal, Ellen Berryman, Kim Cespedes—the most elite women in any category—were there every week.

Ellen O'Neal had this to say about herself and her girl skater peers: "We did not break the mold. We defined a whole new one for ourselves."

A crowded Sunday would see one hundred people or more come to skate and watch. Perennial competitor/commentator David Hackett called the Sunday races "The Fountain of Awesome." Where did I fall in pecking order? Pretty damn low. After reviewing the *National Skateboard Review* archive online, I see that my best race was probably an eighth place—way out of the money and a massive two seconds slower than the winner.

I used to be so bummed out that I couldn't do better, but now I'm fine with it. Because on one sunny Sunday, at a time when it mattered most, I was the eighth-fastest guy in the world.

You're welcome.

Although Team Bahne was the only one with a designated coach, all of the teams had coaching built in. Laura Thornhill said that 1960s holdover champ Torger Johnson mentored the skaters on the Logan team. Torger was Tony Alva's slalom coach, and Tony was a great racer.

G&S had Chris Yandall and Henry Hester.

Bobby Turner's team was already pretty mature, but Bobby mentored them himself.

The Z-Flex guys came a lot; Tony Alva and Jim Muir were terrific racers. Stacy Peralta was a triple threat: good at slalom, freestyle and pool riding. Stacy could put together a winning day whenever he showed up.

OPPOSITE Bobby Piercy. © *Lance Smith/Tracker Archive.*

INSET Henry Hester and Di Dootson surrounded by competitors for the first Hester Series bowl riding contests. Looks like it went over well. © *Lance Smith/Tracker Archive.*

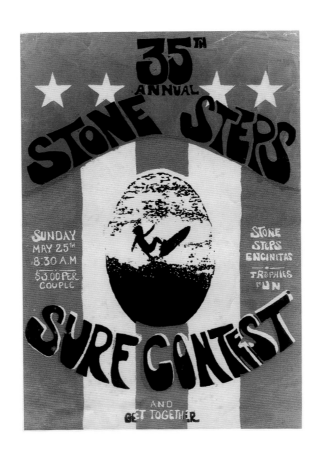

The inaugural vert competitions came right out of Box Canyon.

In 1978, Henry Hester saw that there weren't any pool riding competitions, so H stepped up and created the world's first professional bowl riding contests, the Hester Series.

Since there'd never been a vert contest before, there were no judging criteria; another problem was the Catch-22 that anybody actually qualified to judge the event was competing.

Okay, so a Mount Olympus metaphor is overdoing it, but here's an old photo of a freshly paved Hill where you could race against the best skaters of the day under clear California skies and get clocked by stopwatch or light beam, maybe go home with Tommy Ryan's money. Or maybe leave a few bucks lighter and light-years smarter.

But you know, if Nasworthy hadn't kicked the thing off where and when he did, sooner or later somebody else would have. And then all of this is different. A different time, a different place, different faces. Maybe it drops into Sassy Fox's and Joe Iacovelli's lap in Connecticut years later; they'd have set it up. Or some shred heads in Denmark have an every-Sunday bet designed to snitch gas money off their bros. The Danes would have done a fine job. The Rift feeds you as you pass through: Milk of the Goddess, Royal Jelly, Good Bolivian Flake.

But remove California's jam-packed demographics, perennial great weather and surf industry infrastructure, and I don't see it igniting the way it did.

It's been floated that there were these equivalent regional pockets of hot skaters all around the country that went unreported, which sounds real nice, but nobody's ever showed up with four years of race results or a plethora of pools and pipes. No Alberta Ellen Berryman, no Montana Mikey Williams, no thousand-acre racecourse, nowhere.

In hindsight, I'll bet that them La Costa–Nostra gangsters never had a clue about the standing Sunday wager going on in their town every week, because if they did, they'd have wanted their vig.

OPPOSITE, TOP The original poster for the Stone Steps surfing contest. Just like a regular surf contest, but you had to drink down a bucket of beer before your heat. *Richard Dowdy.*

OPPOSITE, BOTTOM This is probably a final heat one year, Dale Dobson and Donald Takayama are both in it, and everybody looks pretty drunk. *Richard Dowdy.*

"ALL THE BEST THINGS IN LIFE ARE FREE"
(— GALLAGHER + LYLE)
"STAY YOUNG"
ART BREWER
XXX A PERSONAL
FAVORITE
W.B.
CAMERA SCALE /001
JOB
MILES / SEPT. 77 / PHOTO ART BREWER 10/11

Warren Bolster, at the top of his game, 1977. His magazine has 2.2 million readers a month and he's surfing well enough to have a professional rank of forty-fifth in the world. *Art Brewer*.

WARReN BOLSTeR

W arren Bolster came to the craft of action photography as a terrific surfer. That's good enough to surf competitively and good enough to have a professional ranking of forty-fifth in the world in 1977—the same year his own publication was generating two million readers a month.

I hit on this first because being a good surfer sharpens you up for the job of action photographer better than anything else that there is. And because I believe that if someone was to write a few lines about Warren, despite all of his other accomplishments, he'd like it to be those.

Born on June 11, 1947, Warren Edward Bolster was the adopted son of Edward and Elizabeth Bolster. A ranking member of the U.S. foreign service, Edward was the American consul general to Australia.

As the children of career diplomats, the Bolster siblings were extremely well educated, imbued with good behavior and lived much of their lives at high embassy station, enjoying a top-down view of the world. Consequently, Warren could comport himself nicely and was a really polite guy, gracious and generous.

Edward Bolster's embassy postings brought the family to what was a progression of dream locations for any aspiring wave rider.

First stop Australia. Australia in the mid-1960s was a terrific place to take up surfing, with its abundance of great waves and Aussie enthusiasm for surf competitions and for surfing as a national sport.

Warren jumped in with both feet—and a splash. He'd arrive auspiciously at the beach each day, chauffeured in the consulate limousine, complete with little American flags flying on the fenders. The toll collectors along the route were required to salute as they drove past. Warren began to surf competitively, take photographs and write articles about surfing at this time.

Next, the Bolsters were stationed in Hawaii. Hawaii sporting the best waves in the known world and the proving ground for every young-buck surfer with an axe to grind. This is where Warren's surfing and contest repertoire really sharpened up.

After moving to San Diego, Warren had quick success getting published in the surf magazines. As a self-taught photographer, he rose rapidly through the ranks of freelancers to the coveted position of staff photographer at *Surfer Magazine*.

Bolster said that after he arrived at *Surfer*, journeyman surf photographer Steve Wilkens took Warren under his wing, taught him how to tell the big story and turned him into a photojournalist.

Warren's bona fides include a zenith of photographic techniques to portray action, his application of which is rarely surpassed.

- Fisheye captures of surfing and skateboarding just a hairbreadth away from the lens
- Front-fill flash to make his subjects pop
- Adoption of ultra high-speed motor drives
- Chartering helicopters to get an aerial view of massive swells
- Panning with the subject to freeze the rider in space and blur the background illustrate speed
- Strobe shots to illustrate the rider's path in freeze-frame
- His 50/50 series: images snapped as a breaking wave covered exactly half of the lens, showing half terrestrial and half subaqueous
- Remote-controlled cameras with custom mounts to get the view over the rider's shoulder.

Photography projects so esoteric and extreme as to stun his contemporaries, said Steve Pezman, publisher, *Surfer Magazine* and *Surfers Journal. You can only wonder what his peers thought.*

In between shooting surf photos in the 1970s, Warren began to document Skate's new groundswell in Southern California. It was Warren's dazzling images and his vision of skateboarding as a new, surf-centric sport that launched *Skateboarder Magazine* and landed him the job of editor and head photographer there.

It's impossible to know just how and when skateboarding would have evolved without Warren Bolster. Warren's contribution to Skate is primary, singular and absolutely essential.

It was the power of Warren's images, always presented within the tradition and dignity of surf culture, that seduced the U.S. public and the mass media and showcased the sport to an international audience. Go back and read the first issues of *Skateboarder Magazine*, and right there you have 90 percent of what Skate is actually about. And nothing's really changed, except that the kids have gotten so much better.

For the earliest issues, Warren and Craig Stecyk were responsible for creating almost all of the content. Craig used a handful of pen names, so while it might have looked like a lot more people were working on the magazine, it was basically just the two of them at first.

Warren and Craig had the same set of skills: both great photographers, both good writers, both could turn out large quantities of high-quality—even groundbreaking—work on deadline. They were, however, polar opposites in style. But it's just because of this polarity that those early issues have had a time-release effect on our culture that continues to shape it today. Initially it was the allure of Warren's brilliant Kodacolor action shots that seduced the U.S. public, then the international media, and launched the sport worldwide. But it's been Craig Stecyk's mythic stories and photos about Santa Monica's Z-Flex skateboard team, reprised thirty years later in films by director Stacy Peralta, that have blossomed in the post-punk imaginations of a new younger generation.

Warren portrayed the expanse of the sport. He always had his ear to the ground for new talent and new terrain to shoot. He found huge, empty pipes in the middle of the Arizona desert. Nose forever in the wind, he found even more empty pipes, these belonging to a nuclear reactor and guarded by Marines on the grounds of Camp Pendleton. He shot abandoned pools with the best skaters in the world in backyards all over and consistently delivered cool locations and great action to readers throughout his four-year tenure at *Skateboarder*.

And look, it's almost unheard of to build a magazine around a single creative entity the way Surfer Publications set up shop around Warren as chief photographer/editor.

But you know something? Good for them, because while everybody else in the world hoped and prayed for skateboarding to morph righteously from fad to sport, Warren had a top-down vision of what that looked like, and more importantly, he had an actionable plan for getting that done. In just

Pull way back on this photo and it's just a
kid doing a nothing kickturn on a teeny
banked turn. But in Warren's eyes, it's
world champion Laura Thornhill caught in a
moment of grace on a sunny afternoon at
Carlsbad Skatepark. *Warren Bolster*.

two supersonic years, *SkateBoarder* had a global readership of a couple million people a month.

SkateBoarder Magazine was a dazzling thing in its day and mile-high better than any other specialty sport mag. The inevitable knock-off magazines that cropped up in the wake of *SkateBoarder*'s success were predictable teen-zine imitations that folded fast.

Warren was extremely generous in his support of a LOT of people, but he also had this uncanny radar for true contribution that was objective and inclusionary. He presented us with the great and the small of the sport and straight-armed the guys just trying to buy their way in. I think that it's important to understand that in the beginning *Skateboarder Magazine* was the sport, and Warren was the magazine. Nasworthy may have launched the Revolution, but it was Bolster who got the word out.

On the bleeding edge of the bleeding edge, Warren smashed his bones on the foundation of the sport; speaking about his role as spearhead of a new sport, Warren said this, "I almost destroyed myself." The fatigue of his tenure at *SkateBoarder Magazine* and injuries sustained shooting action in the ocean, resulted in a dozen or more surgeries. This and substance abuse sabotaged his career later on. A bad joint replacement triggered falls, causing broken ribs, a broken collarbone and a host of other disasters. He battled chronic pain and became addicted to painkillers and alcohol.

When your job description has "elite swimmer" on the first line and you're stuck on shore watching the movement that you started spread through the gravity sports universe, it will break your spirit after it's broken bones. In 2006, Warren was badly injured in a car accident. Nine days later, on September 6, 2006, unable to cope with the excruciating pain, he took his own life.

Twice married and divorced, Warren is survived by his sister Janet Tramonte and two sons, Edward and Warren Jr.

The talent that one finds around extreme sports circles is just awesome; most of these flying folk are also musicians and artists and designers of the funnest toys in the world. But as rare and wonderful as it is, talent is never in short supply. But true vision like Warren's we see once or twice in a lifetime—maybe. And implemented so powerfully? Maybe never.

As if in answer to Steve Pezman's musing over what Warren's peers thought about his creative output, Jeff Devine, one of surf photography's elders, said, "He really was one of the greatest surfer photographers of all time."

Surfer's Journal published a beautiful coffee-table retrospective of Bolster's work—you should go to the website and buy one right now. Seriously, go there now, this'll keep.

TOP I remember the first time I saw Warren surf, thinking to myself, "He said that he was from Virginia, but he surfs like he's from Hawaii." Right on both counts. Raised in Australia, then Hawaii, THEN Virginia, Warren had the command and aplomb on a board that you see with someone seasoned in substantial surf. *Art Brewer.*

BOTTOM Photographer Warren Bolster in a smooth carve for the camera. *John O'Malley Archive.*

Laura Thornhill top turn, Lakewood Skatepark. *Warren Bolster.*

Virgin run. The first time a skatepark
was ever ridden. It worked like a charm.
Lance Smith (*left*), me (*center*) and
Kingfish. On a hunch, Warren Bolster
showed up just in time to document it.
Warren Bolster.

THE ACTUAL MATH-MATH

Just after Oceanfest in 1975, Jack Graham walked into our yard, came right over to me and said, "John, they say that you're the best skateboarder around." Being blissfully unaware that Bruce Logan and Gregg Weaver lived right around the corner, I told him that, yes, I was.

Now this would be unequivocal had we still been home on Long Island. Mark Hurd, Jimmy Gough and I had dominated the New York skateboard contests during the mid-sixties. Pick a year, and one of us was New York State champ. My family lived on a cul-de-sac with perfect new pavement, so I practiced all the time.

In accordance with the "Market Research" chapter of the trusty Jaycee handbook, Jack had done his due-diligence research to find the best local skateboarder by polling every surfer he knew—which amounted to the three other guys in our household—and so as far as everyone knew, I was the guy.

Sorry, Bruce. Sorry, Gregg.

Then Jack tells me about a news piece he saw about skateboarders being chased out of a tier park in downtown San Diego. They would take the elevator up to the top and then skate down fifteen floors (this is a *lot* of fun).

It was Jack's thought that if one built a place for them to come to and skate, they'd pay to use it.

Absolutely, was my immediate reply. *And I know EXACTLY what it should look like.*

And we were off to the races.

Forty years on, creating the first skatepark might sound like a rinky-dink enterprise, but it was really difficult to do it the right way, and after having worked on other skatepark projects in recent years, I'm here to say that it has not gotten any easier. There's been thousands of skateparks built since 1976 that run the gambit from heavenly to pathetic; in recent times, we've seen about a hundred new skateparks a year in the United States alone, virtually all of them built by municipalities.

Cities are methodically installing our concrete churches.

Find the temple and church metaphors over the top? Tell me about the brotherhood of the monkey bars, your sisterhood of the seesaw.

I understand that today the name *skatepark* seems like the no-brainer term for what to call them, but trust me, there were plenty of cheesy options to wade through. Like *rinks*, *skateways* and *skatercross*—skateBOARD *parks* and *ranches* were tossed around as well. Early on, Jack and I agreed to use the term *skatepark*.

So what?

The point is, that at a time before these things actually had a real name, *everything* was unknown.

Like the money part.

Are there enough kids to sustain a commercial skatepark long-term? How far would they travel to skate? How much would they pay?

Like the dealing with the grownups part.

There was just no good reason for a municipality to approve a zoning variance for a sketchy new whatchamacallit because the probability of a skatepark becoming an eyesore or maiming one of the town's children was just too high.

Like the insurance part.

Who was going to insure something like this? Why take that risk? Would it be affordable?

There was a long list of unknowables, but the most important thing to us as we began was the math.

Not like the money-math. The actual Math-Math.

How to predict speed? How much G-force was safe? What was optimal?

So our initial work—Jack's initial work—was to develop the formulas for determining the falling speed of skateboards, the friction coefficient of skateboard wheels and predicting G-force.

OPPOSITE Bob Biniak, kickturn, Carlsbad Skatepark, with Tony Alva coming up from behind. Neither has a helmet on, so it must be early days. *John O'Malley Archive.*

Using a borrowed radar gun, we did field studies to measure the speed of skaters on flat and banked surfaces. The formulas that Jack developed accurately predicted velocity and G-force.

Because you needed that just to begin a grading plan, right?

Naaah. All of the earliest skateparks left this part up to chance and mostly sucked on account of it.

Modern cities are figuring out that skateparks are a better ride for their recreational buck. They accommodate *way* more users per square acre than a ball sports facility.

A baseball field, for instance, requires a groomed three acres, accommodates two teams and is used just a few months out of the year.

A quarter-acre skatepark handles twice that crowd year-round, in tight rotation, and they're perfect for everybody. Boys and girls, young and old, will all use the right mix of skating terrain.

And I'm sorry, but the notion that baseball is our national pastime is nonsense—watching TV is our national pastime. After Little League, actual participation in hardball falls off the cliff. And when you're wearing a good helmet, Skate life is way safer for your brain than football life.

Why'd we build those first skateparks the way we did?

In early days, the terrain being skated was mostly streets, drainage ditches, paved banks and the odd dry reservoir. Pool skating was still pretty rare. It was these original shapes that informed our concept of what to build, so the first skatepark layouts were all pretty snake-run-y and reservoir-y. Also, early attendance at commercial skateparks was so heavy that flow-through elements like snake runs, half-pipes and ditches were favored because they handled crowds the best.

Since there was no precedent for skatepark design yet, I studied the sculptors Henry Moore and Constantin Brâncuși and the Italian structural engineer Carlo Guidi, then mashed that up with these water conveyance forms, and that was a good way to start.

SNOW FORMS FORGOTTEN

Skateboarding's big daddy may be surfing, but its nutty uncle is skiing. The alpine influence on the sport is largely forgotten today. Remember? Logan Earth *Ski*, Turner Summer *Ski*. In retrospect, Carlsbad Skatepark still looks different than most skateparks that have come since: very organic, part ski run, part waveform, it appeared to just grow up out of the ground.

It's been floated that having Carlsbad Skatepark on the grounds of the Carlsbad Raceway was the extreme sports version of the Tate Modern next to Fenway Park. Now, I've never been to Fenway, but being on the raceway property was invaluable for a ton of reasons.

Originally, Jack wanted to build the park on a doggy piece of property that he owned inland a ways, but when that location failed to pass muster, he thought to reach out to Larry Grismer, the owner of Carlsbad Raceway, whom he'd met in a previous real estate deal.

Carlsbad Raceway was the regional headquarters for drag racing and motocross in Southern California and world-renowned for hosting the Hang Ten World Motocross Championships, a popular event, broadcast on ABC's *Wide World of Sports* every year.

Larry loved the skatepark idea right from the get-go, and while Larry's a good businessman and all, Larry also knows fun when he sees it, and he saw this as some *very* big fun on the way to making some money. It was Larry Grismer who would actually provide all the crucial pieces that we needed to begin:

- **A Zoning Variance.** Situated on the easternmost border of the city of Carlsbad, the raceway was already zoned for all this other dangerous stuff, so the city was inclined to let us do whatever we wanted. Plus, how much more dangerous could it be than *drag racing*?

- **Insurance.** We simply got the same policy as the raceway. It was expensive, but it was a fast, wet-wired deal—besides, there were zero other options. Nobody wanted to be the first guy to insure some sketchy new whathefuckisit.

- **The World Championships.** Later that year, we'd negotiate a deal to host the Hang Ten World Championship contest at Carlsbad Skatepark. Since both the network and the sponsor, Hang Ten, had an existing relationship with the raceway, everybody was comfortable shooting there, so the deal was fast-tracked.

The raceway was set into a natural amphitheater—a California arroyo that offered an overhead view of the moonscape terrain as you arrived, enhancing the skatepark's mystique. It was like a mini moon landing every time you arrived, plus there was this *Field of Dreams* vibe to it. You know… we built it, and they came.

Carlsbad Skatepark was developed in two phases. For the first phase, three elements were originally planned: the Beginner Area, the North Run and the Canyon Run. These last two did not get built.

Widely photographed, the Beginner Area was an organic surf/ski design that was infectiously fun—like good, consistent, small surf. The North Run design was a high-speed, large-format, long-distance bobsled kind of run. The Canyon Run was to be a naturalistic surf/ski environment. It was actually the cost of fencing these long-form banked turn elements that moved them to the back of the agenda.

I believe that push-track layouts have solved this nicely by offering long-format rides on compressed, circuitous courses.

When you're building something new, odds are that the tools you need don't exist, so Jack built ours. The night before we broke ground, he was up all night in his workshop, cutting and welding these new curved stainless-steel blades for the grading equipment, his welding mask lit in strobes by heliarc lightning as he worked.

Jack's new blades bolted onto the machinery perfectly and worked like a charm, enabling us to cut complex curves into the ground fast and smooth.

The procedure for building a skatepark is unchanged today—you sculpt the earth to the shape you want it, then pave over it. Once we started, construction moved quickly. Jack had put the word out for the best concrete-finishing crew around, and when the guys showed up to pave our moonscape, it touched their artist hearts. Their best work was requested, and superb work was delivered.

One of us slept there at night during that week while the concrete was drying so that nobody would try to ride it before it had hardened.

On the first day that the pavement *was* dry, Warren Bolster followed his intuition and arrived just as we were about to skate. He documented us riding a skatepark for the first time ever.

A shot for the ages.

OPPOSITE Considered the embodiment of surf/skate style merge, surfer Larry Bertleman laying out one of his patented Bert slides on land. *Warren Bolster.*

Carlsbad Skatepark, mid-construction.
Kingfish (*left*), Jack Graham (*center*) and me.
John O'Malley Archive.

The skatepark was a ton of fun to ride and worked like a charm...like a poem for you to roll on. We hustled to get the fence up and start selling tickets.

Carlsbad Skatepark opened on March 3, 1976, to great expectation and fanfare. It is meticulously documented in film and photographs. Opening day was attended by the best skaters of the day—Tony Alva, Jay Adams, the Logans, Gregg Weaver and Kim Cespedes were just a few.

About the equivocal term of *original* around the invention of skateparks: there's whispers of prehistoric "skateboard rinks" from the 1960s, and I'd really like to believe that there were, but there's never been photos and I've never met anyone who attended. Maybe there was an effort both dinky and rinky—even by failing fad standards. However, even a marginal attempt would have been widely attended and reported, and photos would exist. Maybe this is a "skateboarding rink" in the same way that a string and two cans are a telephone.

Finally, for decades now, it's been a cottage industry to periodically backdate the opening of a crappy skatepark in Florida for first-ever bragging rights.

This is unsubstantiated nonsense. Total fake news.

The notion that a skatepark built anywhere in the United States in 1976 would possibly go overlooked is implausible, especially in such a huge surf-state like Florida; word just spread too fast. And besides, I rode that place, and it was an absolute waste of good concrete.

How bad was it?

Bad enough for an *alternate universe exercise:*

In a parallel universe, where the clocks run sideways, our Florida poser-park actually *is* the first skatepark ever built. But because it sucks so bad, it opens to a fanfare of broken kazoos and broken hearts and everyone goes home annoyed. It actually sets the whole thing back.

Why do I care? Because if you repeat a lie often enough, it becomes conventional wisdom; eventually, people believe. And because I've had it with listening to this capricious horseshit. I recently saw a Dry White Toast posting online randomly backdating their poseur park opening to January 1976.

Honestly, until someone shows up with some tangible proof, like an original copy of the gas bill or something, kindly STFU and STFD.

The reason it took a full year after the new equipment and inventions came along for the first skateparks to be built is because they're really hard to develop—and nobody else did that, not for a while anyways.

Jack and I understood when we undertook building Carlsbad Skatepark that we were setting a precedent and needed to get it right, so what we did was make a first little iteration that was skateable, profitable and fun. That small first step.

And because, skateparks—above all else—legitimize skateboarding. A place to call home. An address that we hold for you in our hearts.

We'll see you there then, okay?

It was originally the plan to use our buzzing new business to add a little leisure time to our lives, like taking off alternate weekends to go fishing, or surfing, but that never happened.

With an inordinate amount of publicity for Carlsbad Skatepark, in very short order, we'd contract to build a half-dozen more skateparks, beginning with the iconic Concrete Wave Skatepark in Anaheim.

And between ticket sales and design commissions, cash flow was strong and steady. The future was very bright.

Artifacts from Carlsbad Skatepark reside in the permanent collection at the Smithsonian Institution in Washington, D.C.

Me, Central Arizona Water Project.
Warren Bolster.

THE BIG BAG OF COCAINE

The R&D excursions the we took probably look different than your average company junket. Ours were road trips to a hole in the ground.

Among these were a few trips out to the huge full pipes that were part of the Central Arizona Project (CAP) outside of Phoenix.

The last one got a little crazy.

The Central Arizona Project is the largest and most expensive aqueduct system ever constructed in the United States. It's funding was buffaloed through Congress by President Lyndon Johnson in 1968 in order to: "Bring Arizona's fair share of water from the Colorado River."

Construction began in 1973. The water is conducted largely by canal, but some good portion of it flows underground through a perfectly smooth concrete pipe twenty-odd feet in diameter. However, construction on the CAP was halted for a time when the recession dried up its funding.

This left a miles-long underground pipeline exposed and additional random sections scattered about the desert. It was like some magnificent Brigadoon/skate dream.

God, as previously discussed, is truly great.

You could ride the buried portion of the CAP continuously until the light ran out or, if you preferred, skate the unassembled individual links lying around on the ground.

We'd come here a few times, and I liked the long pipeline more than the free-standing links. And it was on my last run, in that grand tunnel, on a sunny Sunday, at just past eleven o'clock, that I fell from the roof of that pipe, landed right on my face and broke my front tooth in half. This caused immediate, excruciating pain.

As you know, dentists are all closed on Sundays, but Don Sheridan, who'd made the trip with us, had a family friend who would patch me up off-hours today, but he was five hours away on the coast. So we packed up fast, made a pit stop for a half pint of whiskey and hit the freeway heading west at warp speed.

Now, I'm not real boozy. I don't advocate drinking and driving, nor do I believe that I actually have a higher pain threshold after hoisting a few whiskeys, but this thing hurt like a motherfucker, so I was wide open to pain-relief solutions. We probably got the idea to anesthetize with booze because that's what they do in the movies—you know the scene in the show where they get some poor bastard drunk, give him a stick to bite on and then saw his leg off quick as a bunny. So I probably looked at the whiskey like a flaky pain management plan B.

However, as expected, plan A, the big bag of cocaine, worked like a charm.

Cocaine is historically used as a topical anesthetic for oral application and is some kind of grandfather to Novocain, which of course is the reason that we kept it handy. I just dabbed a little coke onto the exposed nerve with my pinky and viola! As far as I could tell, it did not seem to impart a debilitating buzz.

On Sunday night, westbound traffic to the coast is predictably heavy with the Sacred Armada of California pleasure craft headed home to harbor after a weekend getaway on their fair share of the Colorado River. The road is packed with motor homes and contractor pickups towing massive campers and boats, all making for the coast at about seventy miles per hour.

I was piloting the company El Camino, which had the biggest engine that Chevy made in 1977, trying to keep our speed to a discrete ninety miles per hour, weaving cautiously through traffic while gingerly dabbing coke onto my tooth and nipping on the whiskey as prescribed by, you know—the movies.

Whoa, this might just work.

Mmmmm…not so fast.

We were on the road maybe twenty minutes when an Arizona state trooper heading in the opposite direction clocked me doing a solid thousand miles an hour and immediately set into the chase.

Fuck.

But he gave me very early warning by immediately flipping his lights on. Now he had to double back to the next off-ramp to make a U-turn, and that was still a long ways off.

Hmmm…

My next exit was still not in sight, so I wasn't exactly sure how to play this. Stopping and speaking with the police seemed like a bad idea, what with the whiskey and medicinal cocaine that we had in the car with us, plus Tommy Kundinger, a minor, riding bitch in the bed of the El Camino, his frightened face now plastered up against the rear windshield.

I decided that an evasive maneuver was the way to go.

My exit was just up ahead, but the trooper was now in my rear-view mirror, lights a-blazin' and closing in fast.

I need to get out of his crosshairs for a minute and stall for time, so I pull up next to an extra-large Winnebago and block all traffic from passing, creating a buffer of vehicles between me and the patrol car. This buys me some time, but my buffer is eroding fast as cars peel away to let the cop pass—all blaring lights and siren, ready to pounce.

As the exit approached, I accelerate ahead of the Winnebago, hop directly in front of him and ease down on my brakes. The motor home decelerates sympathetically, and we slow the entire right lane down to about thirty miles per hour. This gives me sight cover and flushes the traffic in the left lane. I monitor the patrol car in my side-view mirror, and stall… and stall…and stall, until my trooper, now unobstructed, bolts right past me just as I roll right up the freeway off ramp.

But this guy is frosty and catches my trick right away. He hit *his* brakes and swerves into the right lane, tracking my flight in his mirrors.

I come whipping off the ramp and spot an intersection with a shuttered gas station dead ahead. I quick-duck for cover behind the building and peer through the bay doors as my trooper comes wailing up the on ramp the wrong way. But he bets my trajectory wrong and breezes right pass us, heading errantly up the service road. I zoom back on the freeway faster than hell and never look back.

We arrived at the dentist's office very late and very, very wired.

Clay Thomas Whitehead (*left*), his wife,
Margaret, and President Gerald Ford.
Courtesy of the Whitehead archive.

THE TOMS

In America, it's preordained: you invent some shiny new something and you get to parlay it into the Next Big Thing. You take it public, and bam, you're Ray Kroc. Buy a private island. 1+2=a bazillion.

Thank-YOU!

Skateparks were met with the greatest expectations in 1975. It was obvious to close observers that they'd become a permanent addition to the U.S. landscape.

The scent of fresh blood turned the dependably sharky waters of Southern California's fad estuary into a feeding frenzy of con men, each outsized dreamer absolutely expecting to own a piece of every skatepark in the United States, probably the world, forever and ever, amen.

You're welcome.

What'd that look like?

It was a full-time job in our office for someone to answer the phone and listen to callers exclaim: *It's the next McDonalds!!!* Then "uh-huh" them while they insist we execute a get-rich-quick scheme on their behalf, starting today.

A skatepark is the sum of about 6 percent skatepark and 94 percent everything else: money, real estate, municipal approval, design, insurance and OBSCENE amounts of time. Then if you're really lucky, one day: construction. Maybe. So with the goal of creating a chain of first-class, profitable, commercial skateparks across the country, Jack and I set out to find suitable partners. We needed guys who were smart, understood politics and had the money to roll something like this out. So we really lucked into meeting a pair of extraordinary guys for partners. That one of the men was a recent member of the White House senior staff underscores the highest expectations for skateparks that was in the air.

They were Dr. Marshall (Tom) Rockwell and Clay Thomas Whitehead, PhD (also known as Tom). And they well merit introduction here.

CLAY THOMAS WHITEHEAD

Tom Whitehead served as the White House director of telecommunications for President Richard Nixon. As Nixon's presidency began to implode, senior advisor to Vice President Gerald Ford Philip Buchen approached Tom and said that arrangements would have to be made now for Ford's ascendancy to the presidency.

Buchen understood that Tom Whitehead was an organizational genius and drafted him to head the transition team that safely eased the government between the Nixon and Ford administrations.

The team met secretly at Whitehead's home in Georgetown to plan the transition. Also, since Ford had not run for president, he needed the agenda that all presidents require, his so-called black book of platforms; this fell on Tom to curate.

So what?

It was Whitehead's Open Skies policy as communications director that relinquished government control of the satellite system and stopped the FCC cold. Open Skies is what enabled cable channels in the thousands and set the stage for contemporary cellular phone service and internet connectivity. Tom didn't invent satellites, cell phones or the internet, but he envisioned it all, then created the policy that enabled it all to happen.

So, no Clay Thomas Whitehead, no Syfy channel and no cheap cellphone in your pocket.

You're welcome. Now go call your mother.

Do it now. This will keep.

Whitehead held four degrees from MIT, and he taught at Harvard, but Tom also had this whimsical streak just below the surface. It was probably this part of him that loved the notion of a satellite system of skateparks across the United States.

Tom Whitehead passed away in 2008.

Please continue on your own with a Google search on Clay Thomas Whitehead. There's a whole 'nother book out there to be written on Tom that's way nobler than this one.

MARSHALL "TOM" ROCKWELL

But don't bother Googling Tom Rockwell, there's next to nothing. What follows is just my recollection on Tom No. 2.

Tom held a PhD in mathematics and was working at the RAND Corporation, where he met Tom Whitehead. After leaving RAND, Rockwell got his MD, which was something of a family business, if memory serves. Both Tom's father and grandfather were physicians.

The most significant testimony for Tom No. 2 comes from partner Tom Whitehead. With all the geniuses he must have met at MIT, RAND, Harvard and the White House, Whitehead said that Rockwell was among the very brightest.

Tom Rockwell had a graceful way in the world and something of an aw-shucks manner that made working with him a pleasure and a privilege.

He had the ability to digest huge amounts of disparate information drawn from far-flung references and boil it all down into these wonderful, definitive briefs, with everything composed perfectly in the first draft.

Tom Rockwell and his wife, Jenesta Janzen, were partners in Janzen, Johnston & Rockwell, a medical staffing company that supplied emergency doctors and nurses for the Los Angeles area county hospitals.

This is ginormous cash flow and sufficient downstroke to attract the interest of investment bankers, where Tom R. had begun to look for money large enough to fund a big, fast rollout and then take the company public.

How'd we meet? Tom Rockwell's young son was a skater and had been traveling from LA to our skatepark quite a bit; this piqued Dr. Rockwell's interest, and he came along to watch, then contacted us.

In much the same way when your kid gets interested in trains you go all-in and build a train room, Tom's son was a skater, so he'd build the boy a dozen fine skateparks.

It was Dr. R who came up with the terrific new name for the company: Sparks Skateparks. It was also Tom's idea to purchase a plane, cover the cost

by chartering it and use it to get people around fast. I thought that this was a terrific idea—then I took my first ride on it.

Just as we predicted in 1975, today there is a skatepark within driving distance of you anywhere in the states. Unfortunately, this is a *free* skatepark that you don't have to pay me to ride. Oy.

OPPOSITE Portrait of a big-picture guy: Tom Whitehead (*above right, photographing*) taking it all in. Below in the shot: another one that got away, the high-speed Carving Bowl. *John O'Malley Archive.*

ABOVE Jumping the gap between two pipes, Camp Pendleton. © *Lance Smith/Tracker Archive.*

Way out of bounds, some giant pipes
at Camp Pendleton belonging to
the San Onofre nuclear reactor and
guarded by Marines. © *Lance Smith/
Tracker Archive.*

RaNDY aND LaRRY

What's the difference between a plane crash and a train wreck? A train wreck is over, and bam, you're dead. But in a plane crash, you spend your final moments rocketing toward earth screaming, before you're pulverized and roasted.

With the merger of us and the Toms came the company plane. Not just any plane. A really, really, *nice* plane. It's a twin-engine Piper Navajo purchased from the vice president of the Piper Corporation and so, done to the tits. Think swanky, corporate jet with propellers: super-cushy interior/facing seating/bathroom/bar and, decades before common cell technology, a telephone.

Our plan on this fine Friday is to leave from Palomar Airport, in Carlsbad, California, at 11:00 a.m., pick up Rockwell and Whitehead in Santa Monica at noon and then fly to Mammoth Mountain for a working weekend. Jack's compadre from Alaska, Roy, joined us for the trip.

Now, Jack and Roy are real Alaskan men used to ditching helicopters in the tundra and fighting off polar bears with penknives, so they hop right on the plane. Me? I have to check out our shiny new toy.

So I'm walking around this spectacular thing, and after a minute, Jack pokes his head through the door: "What's up?"

I'm checking it out.

"Okay…get on the plane."

Sure, sure.

Back again at the door after a bit. "Now what?"

This is how I make sense of my world.

"Just get on the plane."

Coming!

Wait…lemme just…

"JOHN!"

Okay, Okay.

"Just get on THE PLANE."

OKAY! Okay….jeez-us.

("Nothing's gonna happen…")

I climb in, and our pilot, Randy, fastens the door shut behind me, but everyone fails to notice the stop-work order that God has popped on top of our itinerary, effective 11:45 a.m.

It's a sweeeet forty-minute ride from Carlsbad to Santa Monica, not a cloud in the sky, and Lord, just a glorious California day. I'm facing forward, looking through the cockpit door and the only one enjoying the pilot's view out the windshield.

Up ahead, Santa Monica Airport welcomes us with blue skies and open arms.

All clear to land!

We approach the runway from the ocean but then fly right over it. Control tower to the right, there's no other plane traffic visible—then Randy takes a fast peek back into the cabin. *WTF?*

We circle around again. Aaaand? The same thing—no landing…the fly-by…then the pilot peek. Something's up, but Jack and Roy, facing south, haven't picked up on it yet.

Third time's the charm. We come around again and helloooo right past the tower—no touch-down. But this time, when Randy does the peek back, he sees that I'd caught on and gives me this futile, the-jig-is-up kind of face.

Ohhh lookie here…Randy is something of a character. Lovely.

All right. What is it?

After a sigh and an eye-roll, Randy does a little tap dance: "Well…you know…it's really *not* your day to fly."

Now, frankly I'm tense and a little edgy from ten minutes of blue-sky fly-bys and pensive pilot peeks, so I get a little testy.

Don't you give me that shit. What's wrong?

"The nose wheel won't come down. We might have to land without it."

I pivot right to Jack and Roy: *Oh, just get on the plane! Oh, nothing's gonna happen! Oh! Oh!* Their big Alaskan balls are beginning to get a little sweaty.

We'd find out later that the problem was a leak in the hydraulic line that controls the nose wheel. The manual override fails for the same reason.

The nose wheel doors are open, and the Santa Monica control tower can see the front tire dangling limp-dickly beneath the plane as we fly by. They propose that we perform a series of jerky roller coaster maneuvers, so as to snap the nose wheel into place where the mechanism self-locks. This does not sound plausible to me, and I decide that this is actually just a flaky plan B, because no one really wants to put plan A on the table right away. Tower would let us know when it works.

And although I find that our useless laps of plan B aerobatics are actually a lot of fun, I'm totally unsurprised when it doesn't work. So, buckle up now folks, because plan A, as expected, just plane sucks.

Plan A, if you already haven't guessed yet, is to fly out over the Pacific Ocean, dump all our fuel and—you know—LAND WITH NO FUCKING NOSEWHEEL. On our penultimate pass of whoop-de-dos, I notice fire trucks racing out along the landing strip, and though I know what the answer is, I still asked the question:

What are THEY doing here?

"Foaming the runway."

Fuck.

"I mean, they've just told us that we're dumping all the fuel, but the fire engines and runway foam are also speaking to me, and what they say is, that the prospect of being the guest of honor at yet another massive gasoline fire, is in the offing."

Fuck me dead.

I'm frightened and I'm angry, so I decide to torture Jack and Roy for treating me like a Cub Scout right before takeoff.

Now I understand that there's a part of me that these grown-up guys inherently trust that might be hard to put one's finger on. And I also believe that they've mistaken this for some kind of *intuition* that I don't actually have. So, I pipe up:

Well you can tell them to just go home because I have PRECOGNITION that I'm not going to die in a plane crash.

Cockpit and cabin get real quiet, and after several contemplative moments, my teeny-balled True Believers lean in: "Really?"

No.

Fuck you, you cheeky he-men. Let's just get this thing done.

But wait, there *is* one bright spot: Randy and Larry.

As luck would have it, the end of the Vietnam War has flooded the aviation market with crackerjack pilots, and ours today, Randy and Larry, are two of them. Normally, there wouldn't be a copilot, but Randy's squad bro, Larry, was in town and came to just tag along.

Later on we'd hear stories of their other maniac stunts, like landing planes onto the back of moving flatbed trucks and stuff.

Randy and Larry are a couple of hotshot-cowboy pilots, and this is their kinda rodeo.

The biggest fear is that we'd impact and flip over. This would happen if we touched down crooked and cartwheeled or if the props snagged the runway and we pitch-polled.

I hold my breath on final approach and watch Randy and Larry play that cockpit fourhand, like Virgil Fox and Keith Emerson improvising "The Crash of the Navajo."

Randy brings her in at stall speed, nose up high. He sets the rear wheels on the ground and shuts down both engines, while Larry, out of the right seat and craning for a view of the runway, holds the nose up and steers the plane arrow-straight.

Randy quickly unbuckles his seat belt, jumps up and leans out over the console. He turns the right engine on and off in little bumps to get the propeller just so.

The airport fence is racing toward us.

Randyyyyyyy??? Randy? Randyrandyrandyrandy...

He calmly does the same thing with the left prop, flops back down, buckles his seat belt, sets the nose down onto the runway and hits the breaks.

Now I'm staring straight down at the pavement, the Navajo is screaming like a harpy and skidding along at a hundred miles an hour.

Since I'm sitting across from the exit, it's my job to get the hatch open as fast as possible. I memorize the IN CASE OF EMERGENCY escape instructions printed on the hatch in bold type.

And then...
there's an event blur and it's
     just as
   if
  I'd
beamed out of that plane
        sideways...
   and I'm au courant, standing outside the Navajo, glaring at the open

hatch with my chest heaving and adrenaline dripping out of my gums. The other guys hadn't even looked at their seat belts yet.

Now the Toms glide up next to me on the runway in Janesta's Mercedes convertible, top down, sunglasses to the sky, with these big-ass grins on their faces. Rockwell chirps up: "Well, you certainly have a flair for the dramatic entrance."

I'm pretty freaked out and snap back:

Hey I almost just got killed right now!

The other guys are slowly beginning to exit the plane. After some funereal back-patting in the hanger, we drive to the Rockwells' place in Santa Monica and hold our working weekend there.

And after work *that* night, I got stupid drunk.

SParKS CaRLSBaD

The second phase of Carlsbad Skatepark's construction began after our merger with the Toms and rebranded as the flagship Sparks Skatepark. We set out to make Sparks/ Carlsbad into a showcase for what was possible in a skatepark; this included a clubhouse with a food concession, pro shop and lockers, all housed in a modular building that was design by noted twentieth-century architect Charles Moore.

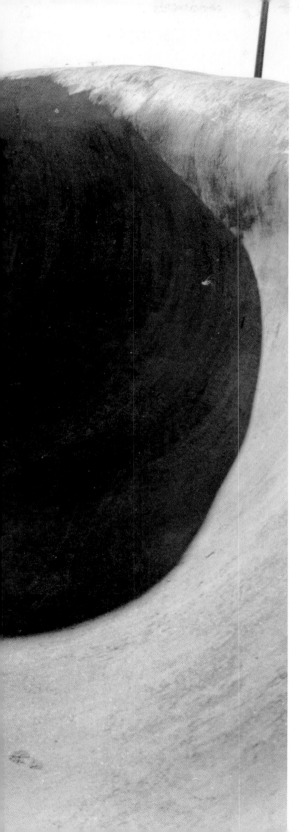

Just like the first phase, the Sparks addition contained three elements. This time, all three were designed and excavated, but then, feeling the cold breeze of the crash of '79 just ahead, only one was paved.

They were:

Tubular Bell, a twenty-eight-foot half-pipe bent into a fat, rounded isosceles triangle.

Carving Pool, an XXL high-speed carving pool/velodrome.

Mogul Maze, a gumbo of the best ski and surf elements that we'd seen, and the one that got paved. We paved the moguls first because it contained something for everyone: approximately one acre jam-packed with the best skatepark features seen to date: a clover bowl, a reservoir, a snake run and past-vert waveforms. It was a zone of unlimited angles.

You could half-pipe all over the place; Rodney Jesse and Gregg Weaver were connecting air transfers and doing past-vert boardslides in those bumps. It was a long-form monolith of integrated transitional elements. Concrete without a comma.

Double overhangs, Carlsbad Moguls.
John O'Malley Archive.

Trust me, if you dug up the Carlsbad Mogul field today, it would be Valhalla for street skaters tomorrow.

But by 1978, the market for skate products was oversaturated. This triggered a market correction in 1979. The Crash of '79 came with an additional whammy for skateparks when their insurance policies dried up.

Here's what happened: The money from the premiums that the parks were paying to shifty insurance brokers was so good that brokers were just running the operation right out of their offices and paying out the rare injury claim themselves. Eventually, the underwriters, who'd been misled as to exactly what they were insuring, figured it out and shut it all down.

When the grand commercial skateparks closed, the kids were put out to play on the streets.

Bye-bye, banked turns. Auf Wiedersehen, vert.

OPPOSITE, TOP Downhill racer John Hughes with Di Dootson in the Carlsbad Moguls. *© Lance Smith/Tracker Archive.*

OPPOSITE, BOTTOM Concrete without a comma. Carlsbad Moguls, partial view. *John O'Malley Archive.*

ABOVE Carlsbad Moguls. *John O'Malley Archive.*

Leucadia Donut Shoppe.
Richard Dowdy.

MaGic-MaGic

And there was Magic. But not like some life-affirming, a-MAAA-zing, kumbaya kind of Magic.
It was Magic-Magic.

BONNIE

Bonnie Wrightsworth was an artist/vendor of ours whose arrival in our midst was a bit startling, so I suppose that I should not have been surprised by anything else about her.

My friend Allen Wrightsworth went away for a meditation retreat sponsored by the Self Realization Fellowship, and when he returned the following week, Allen, twenty-three years old, was married to Bonnie, thirty-two. The two of them about as om-y as a couple of newlywed novitiates could be.

I arrive at the Wrightsworth home today to take Bonnie to proof a job at the printer. Bonnie, the devout SRF congregant, has just completed FORTY DAYS of fasting and meditation—during which time she'd gotten pregnant.

I collect a totally blissed-out Bonnie. But as she settles into the passenger's seat of my beater BMW, Bonnie's gaze lapses deep into the dashboard for a moment, then she looks blankly up through the windshield and, in a small shout, says, "THE CAR'S NOT SAFE. NO! Don't go." Then she turns to me blankly and stares.

Now, I mean, I know that the car isn't exactly safe. *And* I know what's wrong with it. In fact, I'm the ONLY one who knows what was wrong with it.

Next, Bonnie precisely describes the problem to me, tells me where it's located and illustrates it by making a circle with her thumb and forefinger to imitate the shape of the broken flange, then, with her index finger, pokes imaginary holes toward the outside of the circle and explains how the holes don't line up, there's bolts missing and that one is shearing off.

A clear vision of it just appeared to her, and now she was illustrating it on my benefit. As if I already didn't know.

I'm totally stunned by her miraculous revelation, and after a few moments, ask her, *How can you possibly know that?*

Bonnie matter-of-factly explains that her forty-day water fast, meditation and subsequent pregnancy had all served to heighten her natural defenses. The warning vision was just a manifestation of that.

And I'm nodding my head like *sure, sure*, but thinking to myself: *You can rationalize this all you want, but that shit's still supernatural.*

We took her car.

PS: I sold that Beamer to Malvino, and he made the overdue repair. So if you don't believe me about that axle mount, ask him.

And finally:

Dear Universe,
To this day, I'm totally humbled by Bonnie's spidey-sense. Truly, I am. However, I DID drive that old BMW gingerly for another month without catastrophe. And I thought I'd point out that the Cautionary Vision Miracle *sure would have come in handy before, say, the Navajo nose wheel incident. Just sayin'.*

BJ

I smashed my knee up badly in a fall one day, my crappy, state-of-the-art basketball pads doing little to cushion the blow. It was very serious and very painful. It felt like my kneecap had been split right down the middle.

Aikido black belt Curtis Hesselgrave looked at it and winced, and then he offered to take me to the dojo where he practiced. Curtis said that the sensei there, BJ, might be able to repair it for me. I was in really bad shape with no medical insurance, so I was happy for the offer.

Informed of what a martial arts master should look like by the TV show *Kung Fu*, BJ was not at all what I expected. He was a burly, ex-army badass and, despite a pacifist conversion, still looked the part—or at least a middle-aged version of it.

BJ had been a U.S. Army hand-to-hand combat instructor and held black belts in several martial arts disciplines. Curtis explained it to me this way: when you break people up for a living, you have to be able to put them back together again at the end of the day. That's the healing side of martial arts that you never hear about. And so, over the course of his decades of black belts and practice, BJ also acquired the repair techniques of these various disciplines and could readily diagnose injuries by reading the radiant heat emanating from the area with the palm of his hand. It formed an image in his mind of what the injury looked like—a kind of mental X-ray or MRI.

He moved his hand around my kneecap about an inch away from the skin, and after a while, said that I hadn't cracked my kneecap, but I had smashed it badly, inflaming and displacing the ligaments beneath it.

Then he gently manipulated each tendon, sliding them back into the correct position. It felt like guitar strings slipping back into their grooves on the neck. The pain subsided, and the swelling went down. My knee healed quickly and was never a problem again.

You know, I don't care how he came to develop this mental X-ray deal. That shit's still a superpower.

Not buying it? After getting broken up in a bad crash, downhill racer John Hughes was also healed by BJ. So talk to Hughes, if you want. But don't ask Brian Logan. Not long after Brian took his girlfriend there for some repair work, BJ's heat-seeking hands started working overtime, and he started fooling around with Brian's girlfriend.

You're welcome.

Finally, and most profoundly, there was Belva, the Gypsy who'd chart a future for me totally alien from that 1977 life.

But we'll save her story for last.

Tony Alva, Hang Ten contest. *Frame grab from John Malvino footage.*

THE END OF THE BEGINNING

In a sprint past the finish line, just six months after opening, Carlsbad Skatepark hosted the Hang Ten World Championships on September 18 and 19, 1976.

The event was broadcast by ABC's *Wide World of Sports*; Overall Winners were Laura Thornhill and Tony Alva. If you want real reporting on this, there's a complete account of it on the *National Skateboard Review* website, (November '77 issue, page 6) and some clips on YouTube. Google that.

Documentarian John Malvino said that the 1976 Hang Ten contest did a few things:

1. It was the closing quote (") to the "Urethane Revolution."
2. Its coverage by *Wide World of Sports*.
3. The rise of Tony Alva.

First. It was end of those original sod-busting days of invention in Encinitas—we ride the same equipment today. Skateparks are a done deal.

Call it the end of the beginning.

Dos. Of all the large competitions of the day, this was the only one that was covered on ABC's *Wide World of Sports*. This is massive because before today's deep-sport coverage and specialty networks, there was *Wide World of*

Sports and only *Wide World of Sports*. So, it was a huge "get" for both us and skateboarding as a sport.

I think that part of the appeal the skatepark location had was the outdoor setting. Those early arena contests tended to look dingy and claustrophobic on film; also, it was the first contest ever to have a Park Event category—where riders used the banks and bumps to accumulate points for tricks performed. Park, as the event is now called, is a popular standard competition and one of the inaugural events in the 2020 Olympics.

I've pointed you at Di's *NSR*'s website for the real reporting on the contest because my own research netted a decidedly skewed reply from every one of my respondents.

What do you remember about the Hang Ten contest?
Tony Alva's jumpsuit.

Trois. The Hang Ten began the ascent of Tony Alva's career—Alva's effect on fashion and punk rock began in earnest the day Tony became World Champ.

Tony Alva has a few things going for him right out of the box:

The physique of a little gladiator for starters.

Another, the will to push himself farther than anyone else.

And lastly is Tony's belief that on a fair lot of days, he was, in fact, better than everybody else.

Tony Alva was very hard to beat.

Henry Hester may have inched out Alva by a microsecond in the nail-biting slalom final, but pit Tony against the pack? Overall Winner every time.

Tony showed up at the contest that day in a Rolls-Royce and custom rad jumpsuit, both courtesy of millionaire/playboy/surfista Bunker Spreckels. Also in that entourage were Dogtown progenitor Craig Stecyk and other guys who would help launch TA to cultural prominence.

Tony Alva shed his Logan Earth Ski team colors for Bunker's brand-free jumpsuit. He skated, he won, and with the wardrobe change and World Champ title, Tony broke out and became Alva.

Tony Alva's cultural significance was platinum-plated by his consortia with beach culture sultan Bunker Spreckels.

TOP Hang Ten contest. *Frame grab from John Malvino footage.*

BOTTOM Tony Alva (*left*) edging out Henry Hester on right. *Frame grab from John Malvino footage.*

BUNKER SPRECKELS

To the manor born is an admissible hack to begin any bio of surfer and jetsetter Bunker Spreckels. Bunker had an elite and unique pedigree: his stepfather was movie star Clark Gable, and Bunker's inheritance at the age of twenty-one from the Spreckels Sugar fortune made him fabulously wealthy—billionaire status by today's reckoning.

The rarified air of Bunker's world was a blizzard of white powders, and his flamboyant lifestyle of drugs and excess made gonzo journalist Hunter S. Thompson look like a salaryman/piker.

Bunker would be dead at twenty-seven, after six years of envelope-pushing decadence.

If you survey Bunker's life and beneficence, one could make the case that his patronage of Tony Alva was the one that went the distance.

Now, I'm no Bunker scholar (there are those who are), but look at the portfolio of folks who got informal support from Bunker and Tony Alva was the little startup that could—still playing loud and proud into the twenty-first century.

Was Tony Alva Bunker's last stand? Four months after the Hang Ten, Bunker was dead, and Alva launched his own brand, Alva Skates, later that year.

Thanks, Bunker.

OPPOSITE   Stacy Peralta. *John O'Malley Archive.*

Encinitas country style. Encinitas in
the 1970s was much like California
in the 1950s. *Richard Dowdy.*

Even an Eagle

had been up in Long Beach working on an ad campaign with designer Don Sheridan. Our meeting ran late, and I found myself a little wired and having to race home for our 7:00 a.m. crew call.

In an effort to get home fast, I blasted through Orange County and was really leaning on it when I got sniffed by California Highway Patrol radar. A teeny bar of red and blue light snapped on in my rear-view mirror, but it's still waaaay off in the distance and I'm almost home. Also in the rear-view mirror, I notice that my eyes look like huge portals to another dimension.

Oh boy.

I wasn't drunk, and I probably could've lived with a speeding ticket for going 108 miles per hour. However, stopping to speak with the police and maybe having my car searched seemed like a really, really bad idea.

It's 4:30 in the morning, we're the only ones out on the freeway tonight and the race is on.

But the sly duck-and-run trick of my Arizona escape wasn't going to work here.

…not exactly anyway…

That bar of light in my rear-view mirror is getting bigger fast, as the CHP and his eight mighty State of California cylinders close in on me.

I know that I'm outgunned in a drag race, but we're just a mile from home and I think that the new BMW I'm driving can take him in the turns.

Plus, I know the roads.

The La Costa Boulevard exit is dead ahead now, and I come blazing off the ramp before bolting west to US 1. I blow south on the highway through the serendipitously green light and scream down the Coast Highway with a little room to spare. Home is just a few blocks ahead of me now, he still hasn't ID'd my car but he's closing in fast.

As I take my final right up Avocado Street, I'm betting that the officer is not from around here and that he doesn't know these roads like I do, because they all have a real surprise at the end. Avo Street, like all the other streets heading west off Highway 1 in Leucadia, rises steeply for about seven hundred feet, crests, then turns sharply down, terminating abruptly into Neptune Avenue, the bluff road along the ocean, where each intersection dependably has a large patch of sand left by the rain runoff.

I'm banking on stealth and a little sleight-of-hand to facilitate the illusion that I'd just…

Vanished.

I whip up Avocado Street fast as hell; my house is just ahead on the right corner of Neptune and Avo Streets. At the crest, I come down hard on the brakes, cut the headlights and swing neatly into the driveway. I dive into the house and watch from behind the curtains as the cop comes charging over the hill unawares, briefly airborne and blinded as his lights point blankly into the sky.

But the CHP are excellent drivers, and he pulls it off magnificently by fast-braking then sliding sideways through the sand to avoid hitting Walt Phillips's house or launching off the cliff into the ocean.

Not missing a beat, he's out of the cruiser looking for me. But I've just… disappeared. Gone baby, gone.

Had I headed north and for the highway? Or had I ducked south? He surveyed the cars parked about. What was I driving, anyway?

He scratched his head, got back into the cruiser and cautiously drove off.

Even an eagle misses sometimes.

PS: I was really rattled by that close call, not just on my account, but for the cop as well, so I turned over a new leaf. I trimmed my schedule down to an eighteen-hour workday and kept my speed below felony level.

OPPOSITE Stacy Peralta carving the top, Upland Pipeline. © *Lance Smith/Tracker Archive.*

Tom "Wally" Inouye at the
Upland Pipeline. One of the first
aerial sequences ever recorded.
Warren Bolster.

POPSICLE IDOLATRY

I wrote an article in 1978 called "Streetwise" predicting that the decline of commercial skateparks would give rise to street skating, but I couldn't get anybody to publish it.

In 1978, we're jumping out of pipes and skating grand twelve-foot bowls. No one wanted to hear about the end of the party—especially from me—but that's indeed what happened.

A little while back, I was present during a conversation about apportionment of space in NYC municipal skateparks. I was informed that the largest percentage of the facility would be dedicated to street skating elements, because vert was dead.

Huh?

Dude, nobody does this anymore—it's quaint. Deal with it.

This is idiot thinking.

This is like saying that we don't have as many eagles anymore because they're just not as popular. We've cut down the eagle's trees and poisoned the eagle's food.

Vert skating died from loss of habitat, not popularity, you fucktards. Moreover, it seems like we've forgotten that when there were abundant banked surfaces, nobody looked twice at the curbs—kids in Upland got their asses down to the skatepark and spent their time riding full pipe. How is it that our institutional memory is too dim to remember 1978?

Not that you asked, but I've gotta add that there's other stuff missing in your modern skatepark besides vert. Like balls. Street plazas are nouveau,

cheap to build and have been proliferated to pukedom in recent decades; the really great surf-centric skatepark is a very rare exception.

Skatepark designers are remiss here, and I lay it at their feet. And don't give me that *it's what the client wanted* sniveling. Henry Ford once remarked that if he asked his customers what they wanted, they'd say: "A faster horse."

You're on the mound, you pick the pitches and you've been tossing meatballs for decades now. Skatepark development has devolved into a slow-pitch meatball game. Make no mistake about it, banked turns are why we do this.

Need proof? Look at Kona Skatepark in Jacksonville, Florida—open since 1977—with its early snake run still popular forty years later.

A grand snake run in Brazil from 1977 is still ridden and revered. Where's your vanilla street plaza gonna be in *forty* years?

There's a Pinterest page for the twenty best snake runs. Not so much for my twenty favorite curbs.

If down through the decades, every designer had presented, say, a smart, modernized snake run on every project they submitted, the country would

be crawling with them, and since these can be ridden by any type of rolling craft, the whole thing becomes more inclusive—more *democratic*—and much more fun.

One question: can somebody tell me when it became okay to exclude longboards from your skateparks? There's this de facto conceit that a skatepark should be optimized for the common street/popsicle-type board.

This is obnoxious. This is popsicle idolatry.

How about more open-faced banked turns optimized for a longer wheelbase?

How about broadening your horizons?

How about death to popsicle idolatry?

Forty years later, skateboards are the same: minimal and versatile. In contrast, however, the terrain should be expansive, interesting and diverse.

But while the boards today remain the same, with few exceptions, the skateparks are way worse—and I don't mean the workmanship—the quality is mostly high. There hasn't been a unique new skating form created in decades.

Instead, we stamp out these lobotomized street plazas in bare-bones due diligence and think that this somehow absolves us of any innovation.

It's way past time to build new things—roll the dice a bit. Sorry if you don't want to hear that, but innovation is obligatory.

And you know something, when you're saving on the cost of a baseball field and bleachers, you can afford to amortize a little R&D into the process; be bold, be generous.

Do the right thing.

Props to those skatepark designs that leapfrogged the status quo.

Like the Upland Pipeline Skatepark, with its full pipe and huge bowls. That was audacious. Upland went large. Or like the Skatetopia Half-Pipe or the Capsule Bowl. A few guys took calculated risks and pushed the thing higher.

And props to the eighties skaters who were promised great terrain, got fed a lot of nothing and still slogged through.

Two entire generations of skaters—Gen X and Millennials—have grown up in a world of sustained oppression toward skaters, universally run off and equated to vandals. This has produced a kind of Stockholm syndrome among the skating population where even the possibility of a measly knee-high street plaza is met with ecstatic joy and gratitude. You've set your sights entirely too low.

It's time for cities all over to build Olympic-quality facilities. And WAY past time to return to large-format transitional banked-turn forms. Please roll that dice a little. If curbs and staircases are brilliant fun, then almost any intelligent banked-turn solution will be more fun.

My message here? *Wake the fuck up! There's no bars on the windows. You've been free to leave all along. The city is yours.*

And with more active participants than a slew of other sports, you're entitled to have it your way.

Where's the next Capsule Bowl? Tomoca Moon Forest? The next Carlsbad Moguls? A smart, modernized snake run?

Please blend all that stuff with an expanded pump-track layout, optimize the whole thing for a thirty-inch wheelbase, keep all the banks above five feet tall and call me when the concrete's dry.

What, not your cup of tea?

Try it, you'll luvvit.

Final question here.

What's wrong with this picture:

Surfing has Kelly Slater's wave pool throwing up thirty-second-long barrels in the middle of the California desert while the skater market—larger than all its gravity sports cousins, combined, goes begging for the crumbs of short-order municipal skateparks.

This says loud and clear that skaters are miserably underserved by their customized terrain, and this is fixable.

Where do I get off with all this skatepark ranting?

Periodically, we revisit the Original Thought. Take out the Constitution and reread it. Set our watches to Common Time.

I started building skating models as a kid and rode them with little fingerboards.

Waves in the sand, waves in the sheets.

My first *three* skateboards had steel wheels.

In grade school, we built bobsled runs in the snow, for our Snurfer snowboards. In high school, we rode asphalt banks on clay wheels. I built my first skatepark when I was twenty-one.

No one has thought about this longer or on a more granular level than I have.

This is Original Thought. Deal with it.

Rodney Jessee frontside in the Upland
Pipe. © Lance Smith/Tracker Archive.

JANUS COIN

There was a dark side to all that Magic-Magic; there was poison, too. What does that look like?

I've had five friends who killed themselves. I know a couple of murderers.

How many suicide victims do *you* know? How many killers? The usual answer to those questions is NONE, and I sincerely hope that's your answer as well.

The notion of doing something that you love in life calls to everyone's heart. For something really, really fun? Young souls enlisted in brigades for an extraordinary life only to be paid in Janus coin: your beginning and end stamped head and tails.

One day you're making more money than your father and the next day nada. You're left broke, with your head screwed around permanently facing the past.

Short careers focused on velocity over trajectory, undershot Easy Street and landed on the corner of Ecstasy and Abyss Avenues instead.

Welcome home, children. Welllcommme.

I'll let Di unpack it.

In her professional career, Di Dootson was a substance abuse counselor for adolescents, and she spent five years on the front lines of Skate. That's a lifetime of cleaning up the messy lives of troubled kids. She said this: "I blame a lot of the 'adult' sponsors for contributing to the delinquency of minors by encouraging the drug life and thug life which the media just reinforced.

It was negligence, and I see those kids as passive suicides; but I personally never had the authority or the relationship with them to intervene. It's been hard for me to watch."

Stamp Jay Adams's face on the Janus coin for a minute. Jay was the most naturally gifted skater we've ever seen. He beat a guy to death for being gay. RIPs all around.

RULES OF ENGAGEMENT

The rules of engagement are different on the cutting edge. You pay a triple premium for incremental progress—okay, so, maybe we're not exactly curing cancer here—but one still pays in blood. This is true no matter what the chore.

So a little cocaine will cauterize that cut or fuel a long night's work and catalyze those collaborations. Now, a *little* blow has never killed anyone, but a long-term commitment to it always does.

You don't want to hear it? Too bad.

Like it or not, certain excesses occur around extraordinary events. Take the cocaine out of those notoriously snow-blind recording sessions for seminal records like Fleetwood Mac's *Rumors* or Crosby, Stills, Nash & Young's album *Déjà Vu*, and no one really knows how well that turns out.

And since everybody's real happy with the new toys, let's not snicker at a bit of excess that occurred while piercing the Rift.

Now, I am NOT making the case for substance abuse with my Janus view of this mess, but it's worthwhile to note that there were also a substantial number of people who kept the relationship with their catalyst in hand—work-focused folks who have kept innovating and remain standing tall today. And this isn't some druggie rationalization, it's all still here for you to enjoy:

Those great skate toys, them skateparks, four years of excellent issues of *SkateBoarder Magazine*—and the way that *it* changed the world.

An industry, a sport, a new worldview.

You're welcome.

But there were plenty of people who couldn't keep a business relationship with the booze and the blow and worse, and it has taken its toll on my community.

Take the extreme example of TC, a Florida skater whom I was close to. TC's entire family was decimated by smack. Six individuals in all.

During the boom years when pay for TC's skills was good, there was a warm, upward trajectory. But after the skate money dried up in '79, the party raged on and the whole thing went down fast and hard. Drug-related deaths included TC and his brother, his wife, his daughter and two other family members. Some of these were overdoses; some were suicides. An entire family lost to heroin.

How does this happen? As adolescents, TC and his younger brother were abandoned. A family legacy of heartbreak and rejection came to a cold end.

Skating proudly attracts the misfits, the non-joiners. But on the other side of our freak-inclusive coin is disturbing stuff: families broken up by mental illness, poverty, addiction, battering and sexual abuse.

Smart guys like Henry Hester and Stacy Peralta stick up head-and-shoulders above a legion of Jeff Spicolis. Stacy and H came from good homes.

When the dust finally settled in the early '80s, some of the highest-profile bros did a couple years in jail. Of those still left alive today, most are clinging to Jesus and little else just to stay topside.

Not that there's anything wrong with that.

Now, Venice and Santa Monica have always had rough neighborhoods, but worship of the bad-boy ethos cheered kids on to a life past punk into thug.

A woman I know who grew up in Santa Monica in the '80s said that media worship of the radical skate ethos justified a skate-thug superiority complex and thug life shouted over everything else.

Simultaneously, it became okay to sniff at clean-cut guys like Ty Page and Russ Howell shredding in warm-up suits. Ty and Russ are two of the best skaters we've ever seen. You would not have wanted to compete against either of them in their prime.

Fuck you too.

The unsurprising blow-back was that corporations didn't want to partner up with the scumbag life. RC Cola didn't want to brand themselves with criminal poser types? Go figure. Sponsorship money went away and was slooow to return. Bye-bye advertising residual payments.

Flip that coin again.

It's an ironic phenomenon, that from the denizens squatting at the intersection of Ecstasy and Abyss emerged a corps of ministers. This is a handful of skaters who have continued their life's work in service of other souls.

Lane Oaks, Eddie Elguera and Christian Hosoi have their preacher shingles out. To these I'd add Dennis Martinez and Michael Williams, shaping the trajectory of their intentional communities. Steve Schisler holds down the bass in a kickass gospel group.

A little heaven for a little hell? It's a break-even deal maybe, the Janus Coin.

OPPOSITE Mr. Incredible, Ty Page. One of the best surfer/skaters we've seen. *Warren Bolster.*

ABOVE Laura Thornhill top turn, Carlsbad Skatepark, nighttime strobe session. *Warren Bolster.*

Long forgotten skatecar. Signal Hill
race. *Warren Bolster*.

CROSSWIND HURRICANE

Just like when your car is in the shop and insurance picks up the cost of a loaner car, while the Navajo was being repaired, we got a loaner plane. It was a small, single-engine, five-passenger Cessna. When I say "five-passenger," it's probably suitable for three. Picture five big guys in a Yugo. We used the Cessna to return home after the Navajo crash, and we'd continue to use it for later commutes to Santa Monica. But a couple flights had their own terrifying episodes, including one violent landing and a nightmare ride that was way heavier than either crash.

We return home late one night to a Palomar Airport in cloud-black conditions with a vicious crosswind strafing the runway. I get a funny taste in my mouth as we approach and could see that it was going to be a touchy landing.

Randy is really struggling to bring it in square; then, with wheels about twenty feet off the deck, we're slammed starboard by a microburst. It pitches the right wing up and blows us sideways off the runway. Randy muscles us back over the pavement, and we slam down hard on the gear—bounce, hit cockeyed, nick the left wing on the ground and then almost flip over while correcting course.

It was freaking gnarly, and I went home really shaken up.

However, the most bone-chilling episode was passing through a thunderstorm on our way up to LA.

It's yet another fine California Friday, about twenty minutes past our eleven o'clock take-off from Palomar, when Randy and I enter this ferocious gray thunderhead somewhere over Orange County.

Once inside, we're immediately met with hurricane winds and tossed around like a flimsy little toy. Rain strafes the windshield like a fire hose and water pours off the side in rivers.

We are boxed ferociously from side to side then stove straight down hard by fists of microbursts. This sucks the air out of your lungs and the wings of the plane. You free fall, and when the wings finally catch, it feels like you've hit concrete and the force is pounded right up your spine. Traveling at three hundred miles per hour in totally grayed-out conditions, there's no spatial reference, so you're force-fed vertigo. I blink and shake my head to get my brain to snap out of it, but that won't work, and strobes of diffused lightning explode around us in the clouds. Randy is wrestling with the wheel, eyes firmly on the instruments. He yells at me: *Don't worry, the plane is designed to withstand these conditions.*

But this is no reassurance, and I'm not real convinced that Randy was giving me the whole story…again.

I avert my eyes from the windshield, go into my happy place and chant Randy's weak assurance as my mantra: *The plane is designed to withstand these conditions…The plane is…*and while not claustrophobic, I'm about to whip up a seriously bad case.

Then, after an eternity, we pop out the other side, instantly calm and sunny again. I turn to Randy and say, *Look, I'm walking home before I ever do THAT again.*

Our return home was uneventful, but I never set foot in that thing again, or the Navajo, for that matter, when it came back from the shop. I figured that I'd had my three strikes and wasn't interested in pushing my luck.

OPPOSITE The Hang Ten World Championships. A few riders are doing circles around commentator Bud Palmer as he's filmed doing his closing monologue. *Warren Bolster.*

Me kickturn. *Warren Bolster*.

SKaTe as NeXUS

C ut to now, and it's all come to pass.

The hills of La Costa are covered with nice homes. Skateparks sprouting up around the planet.

Skate as Nexus.

Moe Dalitz lived to a ripe old age and died in his own bed. He never did come calling for his vig.

So, my question is this:

Honestly, what are the odds of this all happening?

Of Frank Nasworthy gliding into Nowheresville on his new invention?

Of this harmonic convergence of drought, recession and Mafia chill?

Of these tangents assembling on a hill in Hippie Heaven, tearing open the Rift to the Revolution and drawing a gravity sports universe around it?

Look it's gliding past the house now. *Oh, hiiee!*

Or of a guy like me getting exploded into a genius inventor on the lam from Colombian narcos?

Or of Weaver getting aimed at Nasworthy that day?

Or any of this supernatural shit bubbling out of Omsville for fuck sake?

I'll bet that Moe would make the sign of the cross and give you very long odds on randomness.

In 1977, I was interviewed by *SkateBoarder Magazine* and I made this barf-worthy remark about it all being *Manifest Destiny*. And while this might be obnoxious, it's still true. Come on, how else could it be?

You tell me.

But if this was to be true, my pre-destiny proposition, then it would dependably leave a trace: Fingerprints from the Hand of God.

Some proof.

And lastly, there's Belva, the Gypsy fortuneteller who'd reveal to me the arc of my life.

The future, at hand and away.

I had not been in the market for a good soothsayer, but my friend, the eminent San Diego psychologist Charlie Nelson, recommended Belva to me.

Charlie was at his last wit listening to the secretaries in his office yammer on about Belva's miraculous predictions, so he went for his own reading in order to debunk the mystical water cooler chatter.

Instead, Charlie came away woke by Belva's profound exposition of his life and pointed me at her, scratching his head nonetheless.

I arrive at Belva's door at eleven o'clock sharp, which she notes as she greeted me. *Ah, John. Right on time. Please come in.*

I enter the front room and scan the house.

Belva was certainly Eastern European, unselfconsciously 1950s in her dress and décor and deeply Roman Catholic by the clutter of religious iconography around the house. Jesus, Mary and Joseph, God the Father and the Holy Ghost glare at us askance from vividly rendered statues and paintings.

It was the very familiar Catholic motif that I'd grown up with, applied extra-extra thick.

We move over to her table together and settle in, she across from me.

Belva places a deck of old, worn playing cards between us and says: "Shuffle the cards 'til you're ready, then hand them back to me. Take a pad and write down everything that I tell you. Keep it safe. Cross off the things as they happen."

I cut and shuffle the cards as she said to, then hand the deck back to her. She dealt them out between us on the table. Belva's eyes tear up involuntarily, as she had warned that they might. Then she abruptly stops and looks up at me: "Your music is more powerful than anyone realizes. Even yourself."

This is a pop fly into deep left field to me, because at the time I was just a dependable side-man harmonica player. But I catch a glimpse of *Dreamland*, the redemptive rock opera that I'd channel seven years on and strains of violin I'd take up, still decades away, and took note.

Then she began in earnest:

"Do you want both the good news AND the bad news? Or just the good news?"

Both please.
"Oh, that's fine, because I don't have any good news for you."
Nice.

Then she methodically laid out a horrifically bad five years ahead for me in personal and business fortune.

She called up my friends by name and discussed our relationships intimately. She referenced private conversations—stuff that only I knew. She did not offer up anyone unknown, nor did she tell me that I'd have two children—standard fare among commercial psychics. It was like she slipped inside of me, looked around and discussed what she saw objectively. Di Dootson's housemate Paul had just died. Belva knew this, and she knew his name. She spoke conversationally, never probed and never asked me questions.

She could see to the end of some things, other things not.

I made my list and Xd out each item as they came and went over time.

A life predicted. *Under the action of given forces.*

Destiny Manifest.

There's deeper things at work here.

I crossed off Belva's sweetest prediction recently.

Squinting past the edge of her vision: "You have someone."

Uh-huh.

"That'll work out."

My eyes teared up involuntarily. *Thank you.*

Thank you.

Look, my pragmatic world had holes punched in it by that Gypsy, a sensei with X-ray hands and this clairvoyant pregnant lady. And any business of parsing karma from coincidence is way above my pay grade.

So, you tell me.

What the fuck are the odds?

The Revolution's pouring through your town now. Fun and community buzzing right by the window. It creeps uphill, it gliiiiides downhill.

So, why throw down about it now?

Because I've been trying for forty years now to put this all together to explain to my childhood mentor, Joe Twyford. And because this all has been overlooked for all these decades—that little vein of uranium in the Carlsbad foothills that we never went back for. And because I'm up to my ankles in Dry White Toast crumbs here. And since I missed my deadline with Joe, I thought that I better get cracking.

With the decline of ball sports and organized religion we've seen the ascent of gravity sports. Skate is the center of the gravity sport universe, and skateparks are Skate's temple of that. And because skateparks are the Forward Operating Bases of the Revolution.

There's a girls' skater movement in Afghanistan.

Tribes are formed differently now.

Here is the technology that brought you rolling luggage. Skate changed your life. Free at last! Free at last! From ever having to schlep your shit around anymore. The Revolution is in your closet.

And because we're pre-punk here, punk emerges immediately out of Skate. Out of Craig Stecyk and Tony Alva, from speed demon Terry Nails, pool rider Mike Palm and photographer Glen E. Friedman. Skate fed punk. Punk feeds back. Forever and ever, amen.

And in truth, the only "civilians" left that still recall those 1970s formation days anymore are the old punk guys.

I run into them when I'm out sometimes. They come over and talk; with their arms tattooed in sleeves and their drinking problems, they come over and talk.

Hey man, I remember. I remember how it was... And they tell it all back to me again. It's nice.

At a concert recently, my sweetie came over to me and, shouting over the band into my ear, asked, *"Hey, what's with you and the old punk guys?"*

These are my people.

Me anymore? I get jumpy around eleven o'clock on a fine Friday or sunny Sunday. My antennae go up, and I scan the horizon for another noon-ish disaster that wants to run me down. Crush me, drown me, explode me, for once and for good.

Best advice from me?

I got nothing…other than the obvious: Cash in your coin trajectory side up and, when heading off into the unknown, bring a wizard or a genius along.

It was a lucky day when them Colombian narcos banked wizard/genius Jack Graham off the Aleutian Islands and into Leucadia. The Grahams' ill wind was a new sport's offshore breeze.

Jack would have really dug hearing the news that skateboarding got picked up for the Olympics. Then he'd take a thoughtful drag on his cigarette and wonder what took them so long?

And you know, I'm sorry that he's not here to explain this stuff better than I can and to get the recognition he deserves. You'd have enjoyed having the Grahams as neighbors.

But anyway…for my part?
I interrupt your stream to let you know that

The Rift has opened
God is great
Spread the word.

173

Robin Aloway (*left*) and Tony Alva (*right*),
Carlsbad Skatepark. *Warren Bolster.*

AFTERWORD

So, all of this stuff is true, but I changed some names so as to not injure somebody or piss somebody off. I'm not here to rub anybody's nose in their business.

But do me a favor: if you liked my book, buy a copy and send it to a friend. And if you hated it, buy a copy, send it to a friend and discuss.

Thanks for listening!

—jono

PS: And lastly, if you've followed along and noticed the omission of a promised chapter on naked hippie chicks, sorry, but I lied about that.

This is family entertainment here.

However, if you send me an email to urlostchapter@gmail.com, I'll email you the omitted chapter, which is titled "Killer Pussy."

Enjoy!

GLOSSARY

A&P. Short for "The Great Atlantic & Pacific Tea Company," it was an American chain of grocery stores that ceased supermarket operations in November 2015 after 156 years in business.

Adams, Jay. The youngest and perhaps the most naturally gifted member of the Zephyr skateboard team. He's featured prominently in the 2001 documentary *Dogtown and Z-Boys*.

Alva, Tony. An original member of the Zephyr skateboard team, his *Alva Skates* brand of skateboards is still in production today. Tony is perhaps the most iconic skater of all time.

Arctic Ocean. Located mostly in the Arctic north polar region in the middle of the Northern Hemisphere, the Arctic Ocean is surrounded by Eurasia and North America.

Arizona Highway Patrol (AHP). An American law enforcement agency focused on the protection of the Arizona highways.

OPPOSITE Ellen Berryman, competing barefoot. *Warren Bolster*.

Bahne, Bill. Bill began his career as an engineer designing submarine parts for the U.S. Navy in San Diego. He began shaping surfboards, and early on he invented and patented the removable surfboard fin. That company is called Fins Unlimited. A prolific inventor, Bill also developed the single ski, new skateboard trucks and flexible boards and breakthroughs in the modern-day surfboard shaping machine. He is partners in companies with his brother, Bob.

Bahne, Bob. Bob is Bill Bahne's brother and business partner in all the Bahne-owned companies. Bob runs the business side of things.

Bahne/Cadillac. The entity created from the merger of Cadillac Wheels and Bahne Skateboards.

Ballantine. Ballantine beer is an American beer originally made in Newark, New Jersey.

Balma, Larry. One of the foremost figures in twentieth-century and twenty-first-century skateboarding, Larry is a founder of Tracker Trucks, arguably the first skateboard trucks that enabled skateboarders to push the limits of their gear. Larry went on to create Transworld Publications, a family of about twenty gravity sports publications and websites.

Barranquilla. A city located in northern Colombia. It is the largest port in the northern Caribbean coast of Colombia.

Batiquitos Lagoon. A coastal wetlands and estuary that sits between the La Costa development and the Pacific Ocean.

Bennett, Ron. Inventor of the Bennett Skateboard truck, one of the first to be designed specifically for skateboarding. Ron was an enigmatic character and an exemplary gentleman.

Bennett Trucks. An early breakthrough in skating performance, Bennett Trucks were a quantum leap over existing equipment, with handsome styling and smooth turning ability. The smooth performance of Bennett's trucks was forever dogged by the faulty plastic mounting plates—or base plates—that would break easily. As higher performance skating put more demands on equipment, these good trucks were jettisoned in favor of more dependable equipment.

Berryman, Cindy. Encinitas native, writer, elder sister and sensei to champion skater Ellen.

Berryman, Ellen. A freestyle specialist whose incorporation of gymnastic maneuvers into her routine made her all but unbeatable. Her inverted strength and balance moves have never been surpassed.

BJ. *All right, enough of that*. The nickname of the martial arts master who healed my knee and ministered to numerous others in pain.

Black Hill. El Fuerte Street in La Costa. The first hill where skateboarding became popular.

Bolivian Flake. High-quality cocaine.

Bolster, Warren. Visionary photographer of surfing and skateboarding. Warren was editor of *Skateboarder Magazine* from 1975 to 1979. See his chapter in this book.

Box Canyon. Venado Street. The second and longest-lived location of the La Costa pro skate scene.

Bratz. Cover band working and playing in the North County area in the mid- to late 1970s.

Brewer, Art. Photographer and elder statesman of the action photographer genre.

Cadillac Wheels. The first-ever skateboard wheels made out of polyurethane plastic. The company was founded by Frank Nasworthy.

California Highway Patrol (CHP). CHP has jurisdiction over the California highways and can act as the state police.

Carlsbad Raceway. Regional racing center, host to weekly drag races and motocross. Home of Carlsbad Skatepark.

Carlsbad Skatepark. Designed, owned and built by Jack Graham and John O'Malley, it opened on March 3, 1976, and is considered to be the first skatepark in the world. Reports of earlier skateparks have never been verified.

catamaran riding. Seated sideways on a board, two skaters face each other, interlock their legs and ride downhill together. This gives either more stability or less stability to the act, depending on who you ask. It definitely doubles the fun.

Central Arizona Project (CAP). Home of the legendary Desert Pipes, massive full pipes left scattered after the CAP lost funding in the mid-1970s.

Central States Teamster Fund. The pension fund for labor union the International Brotherhood of Teamsters. Funds from this pension fund were used to build the La Costa Resort and Spa in Carlsbad, California, around which the community also know as La Costa was developed.

centrifugal buzz. The fun feeling you get from rounding a banked turn.

Cespedes, Kim. Pool rider, slalom racer, surfer and tomboy Kim won the slalom division at the 1977 Hang Ten Contest.

COD (C.O.D.). Cash on delivery, or collect on delivery, means payment for goods is made at the time of delivery.

Cousteau, Jacques. Cousteau (1910–1997) was captain of the marine research vessel *Calypso*, inventor of SCUBA equipment and conservationist.

Cousteau, Philippe. Second son of Jaques Cousteau, a diver and cinematographer, he was the cinematographer and director for most of the Cousteau films.

Crash of '79. The market downturn that began in 1978 that execrated the skateboard industry and led to ten years of dark ages for the sport.

Cupertino, California. A city directly west of San Jose and notably home to Apple Inc.

Dalitz, Moe. A mobster and casino owner who parlayed his position in the Mafia to leverage the funds from the Teamsters pension plan into the La Costa golf club, spa and surrounding community.

Deadliest Catch. A documentary TV series that portrays the real-life events aboard Alaskan king crab fishing boats.

Ditch Plains (Ditch Plains Beach). A beach, surf spot and community about a mile east of the town of Montauk.

Dogtown. The area approximately encompassing the California cities of Santa Monica and Venice, location of Zephyr Surfboards and Z-Flex skateboards, as well as the abandoned Pacific Ocean Park amusement park and its abandoned pier, known as the POP pier.

dojo. A room or hall in which judo and other martial arts are practiced.

Dominey, Dave. Dave is a visionary designer and was key in the creation of Tracker Trucks. Dave went on to revolutionize windsurfing and sailboat racing performance with his Streamlined company's urethane universal joints.

Dootson, Di. Di was present at the creation. Tracker Trucks were developed in her house, and she was among the first La Costa skaters. The whole race scene and industry sprouted around her stewardship. See the chapter on Di in this book titled "Betsy Ross-y Stuff Aside."

Emerson, Keith. Virtuoso keyboard player and composer from the rock band Emerson, Lake & Palmer.

Encinitas, California. A beach city located in the North County area of San Diego County, California. It's located about twenty-five miles north of San Diego.

Eng, Paul. Slalom specialist, La Costa racer and Team Bahne member who was known for a fast, clean style. He won the slalom championship at the 1975 Bahne/Cadillac contest.

extreme sports. Recreational activities perceived as involving a high degree of risk. These activities often involve speed, height, a high level of physical exertion and highly specialized gear.

Fenway Park. A baseball park located in Boston, Massachusetts, home to the Boston Red Sox.

Fox, Sassy. East Coast doppelgänger to Di Dootson, Sassy was race director/starter for slalom racing in Connecticut.

Fox, Virgil. A twentieth-century classical organ player who had a sort of rock approach to the pipe organ. He brought his "Heavy Organ" style to the public in concert halls and arenas with a large touring pipe organ.

Friedman, Glen E. Photographer/social documentarian influential in early skateboarding, punk rock and rap, among other subject matters.

G-force. For the purposes of this book, the feeling one gets when executing a banked turn.

glassing shops, or **glassers**. This is the process of wrapping a finished surfboard in fiberglass for strength, protection and water-proofing (see also surfboard shapers).

G&S. See Gordon & Smith

Gordon & Smith (G&S). One of the largest and most successful skateboard companies of the late 1970s, G&S boards first emerged with an excellent slalom skateboard called the Fibreflex.

Graham, Jack Lynn. Diver, boat captain, inventor, visionary. See Jack's chapter in the book.

gravity sports. Any sport powered by gravity, such as surfing, skiing, snowboarding, skateboarding and so on (see also extreme sports).

Grismer, Larry. Ex-pilot and co-owner of Carlsbad Raceway, the regional drag strip and motocross race course in Carlsbad, California.

Gullwing Truck. The first skateboard truck with a "reverse kingpin"— different than what was typically used, several brands make trucks like this now.

Gypsy. Also known as Roma, people originating from the Indian subcontinent. Some are known for a nomadic life, with a penchant for occupations as musicians and fortunetellers.

Hawk, Tony. Skateboarding's most prominent and successful member, known for the most extreme tricks and maneuvers. His video game is one of the most popular.

Hesslegrave, Curtis. A black belt in Aikido, he was a writer for *SkateBoarder Magazine* and brought martial arts techniques of relaxation and rolling out of falls to the magazine's readership. An original La Costa boy, he was a good racer. Curtis also was a master designer and builder (foiler) of surfboard fins.

Hester, Henry. One of the winningest slalom racers of the mid- to late 1970s, and perhaps ever. Henry is a thinking man first, a competitor next and a racer third. Henry also started the first-ever pool/bowl riding contests, the Hester Series. Also answers to H or HH.

Hippie Heaven. My nickname for Encinitas, California.

Hitchcock, Skitch. Surfer, skater and homegrown inventor, Skitch was an excellent freestyle competitor, invented new board types and built the first modular fiberglass ramp.

Hobie Skateboards. Skateboard manufacturer.

Hughs, John. American skateboard speed racer. Original La Costa boy.

Icaovelli, Joe. East Coast slalom racing patron Joe and company held down for slalom racing with their Farm races for over ten years. Joe is bat-shit crazy.

Janus. Janus Coin. Ancient Roman god of beginnings, duality, doorways, passages and endings. He is usually depicted as having two faces, since he looks to the future and to the past. The two sides to a coin.

Janzen, Janest. An emergency medicine physician. Also wife and business partner to Marshal "Tom" Rockwell.

Janzen, Johnston and Rockwell. Engages in the provision of emergency medicine physicians and staffing to hospital emergency departments, among others.

Jaycees. Also known as the United States Junior Chamber, it was established on January 21, 1920. It provides opportunities for young people to develop personal and leadership skills through service to others.

John Deere. An American manufacturer of construction and agricultural heavy equipment. The company's slogan is "Nothing Runs Like a Deere."

Johnson, Lyndon (LBJ). The thirty-sixth president of the United States.

Johnson, Torger. A champion skater in the 1960s and the 1970s, Toger was a great freestyle and slalom skater. Tony Alva said that Torger was the most influential skater in his life.

Kincaid, Tommy. A pseudonym for my co-worker at the beverage depot and the driver of the beer truck that I was almost incinerated in. It was Tommy's brute force that opened the door and allowed us to escape from being burned alive. Tommy, you know who you are. Thanks, bro.

kinematics. A branch of classical mechanics that describes the motion of objects without considering the mass of each or the forces that caused the motion.

Kroc, Ray. The American businessman who built the McDonald's hamburger chain into the the most successful fast-food chain in the world.

landing craft. Small and medium seagoing vessels such as boats and barges used to convey a landing force from sea to the shore during an amphibious assault.

Logan, Barbara. The matriarch of the Logan family of surfers and skaters who lived in the South Bay area of LA.

Logan, Brad. Freestyle and slalom skater from the South Bay area of Los Angeles. A middle child in the Logan family, Brad was a successful competitor who competed and won in both the 1960s and the 1970s.

Logan, Brian. The eldest of the Logan siblings, Brian perhaps bridges the gap between surfers and skaters in a quintessential way as a member of the Bing surfboard team in the 1960s and founding Logan Earth Ski skateboard company in the mid-1970s.

Logan, Bruce. World Champion and the most competitively successful of the Logan sibs. Bruce surfed and skated in the mid-1970s. Perhaps one of the winningest skaters of his day, with twenty-two first-place wins.

Logan Earth Ski. One of the earliest, and then the largest skateboard manufacturers of the mid- to late 1970s. It was founded by Brian Logan and run by his mother, Barbara. The company had the benefit of an early affiliation with Makaha skateboards, a venerable brand from the 1960s, and the high profile of all four Logan children: Brian, Bruce, Brad and Robin.

Logan, Robin. The youngest of the Logan clan, Robin began skating at age four. She was a top competitor as both a freestyle skater and slalom racer.

longboard. A skateboard with a wheelbase of twenty-seven inches or more.

Löwenbräu. A venerable old German brewery.

MacGyver. An action-adventure TV series. It had some big-ass explosions.

Mafia. Also known as the Mob. Organized criminals, originally from Sicily and now in the United States, with a complex and ruthless behavioral code.

Malvino, John. Surfer, skater and filmmaker, John's first skateboarding movie was *That Magic Feeling*. He has contributed to many other films, such as *Dogtown and Z-Boys* and *Riding Giants*.

Mifsud, Louis. My childhood classmate whose example of gymnastic excellence gave me the inspiration to rocket myself out of the burning truck. Thanks, Louie.

Mohr, Bob. Skater, musician, La Costa boy and 1977 World Freestyle Champion, Bob skated his whole career for the Bahne skateboard team.

Montauk Point, New York. Located at the tip of the South Fork of Long Island, Montauk is famous as a summer tourist destination and for its great fishing and surfing. A quaint little drinking town with a bad fishing problem.

Morey Boogie Board. The original finless body board, invented by Tom Morey.

MotoBoard. The first mass-produced motorized skateboard, it was powered by a two-stroke engine and designed by Jim Rugroden. The original company was run by Rugroden and entrepreneur Bill Poesy.

Mount Olympus. Notable in Greek mythology as the home of the Greek gods, representing a pinnacle.

Muir, Jim. Original member of the Z-Flex team. Jim was a good pooler rider and slalom racer. He also ran DogTown Skates.

Nadalin, Ed. A freestyle skater and competitor, Ed and his barefoot approach to skating led him to be featured in many films, commercials, ads and magazine articles.

Nails, Terry. Musician and skatecar racer, Terry was a member of the band Tommy Tutone 2. His final run at the Signal Hill speed race was memorialized when his skatecar failed to brake and went out into traffic, where it was hit by a car. Terry lived.

narcos. The most notable drug lords trafficking illegal drugs, notably heroin and cocaine.

Nasworthy, Frank. Frank introduced the polyurethane wheel to skateboarding. He's rightly considered the father of modern-day skateboarding.

***National Skateboard Review* (NSR)**. A newspaper devoted to covering the grass roots of skateboarding published by Di Dootson from 1976 to 1979. www.nationalskateboardreview.com.

Navajo. Piper Navajo is a cabin-class, twin-engine airplane manufactured by the Piper Aircraft Inc.

Nelson, Charles. Charlie is recognized as a seasoned, direct, warm, ethical, "practical" therapist. According to his bio online, Charlie "believes that most people achieve their treatment goals more effectively and efficiently when meeting with a therapist with a warm, honest, open, intelligent approach blended with a timely sense of humor and wisdom… not dry, confusing, contrived, psychobabble." And also the occasional visit to a witch doctor, by his advice to me ;).

Ocean Fest. Promoted by Bill and Bob Bahne, it was a two-day festival and exhibition of all things gravity sport of the day. Its Bahne/Cadillac contest was the opening bell to the Urethane Revolution.

Oki, Peggy. An original member of the Zephyr team. She is an artist and environmental activist.

Olympic Games. The leading international sporting events in the world. Both skateboarding and surfing were chosen to be included in the 2020 Olympic Games in Tokyo, Japan.

om. A sacred syllable of Hinduism. The syllable *Om* is also referred to as *Omkara*. It is also used as a mantra to chant.

Omsville. My nickname for Encinitas, California, in the 1970s

O'Neal, Ellen. An early professional skater, Ellen was known as a clean-cut girl next door. A terrific freestyle competitor, her photogenic bright smile made her a darling to millions of skater fans.

Ottumwa. A city in southeastern Iowa, bisected by the Des Moines River. It is the county seat of Wapello County.

Pacific Ocean Park. A twenty-eight-acre nautical-themed amusement park built on a pier (POP Pier). After it closed and fell into disrepair, the park and pier anchored the Dogtown area of Santa Monica.

Page, Ty. Uber-talented surfer and skater Ty, nicknamed Mr. Incredible for his rapid-fire technique and footwork, excelled in freestyle slating but was an adept competitor in all aspects of the sport. He won may surfing contests and a junior competition.

Palm, Mike. Founding member, frontman and singer/songwriter for the seminal Orange County punk band Agent Orange. It was one of the first bands to mix punk rock with surf music. Mike was an original bowl skater in the 1970s and something of an amateur historian on the subject of that time and of Carlsbad Skatepark in particular.

Palomar Airport. McCelland-Palomar Airport is a public airport in the southeast part of Carlsbad, California.

Piercy, Bobby. Slalom racer, scoundrel and all-around great guy, Piercy began his career as a ski racer in Colorado. The term *rock star* is always used in conjunction with Piercy. This is not an overstatement. Rumors surround his death; he is thought to have died in a swimming accident.

Peralta, Stacy. Original Z-Boy, skater, surfer, director, writer of a documentary and fictionalization on Dogtown and Z-Boys. Stacy was also partner in the skateboard and accessories company Powell Peralta. Stacy is one of the most versatile and influential skaters ever.

point break. A wave that is most suitable for surfing, which breaks sympathetically around a point of land. A right-hand point break is one that breaks headed right from the perspective of the rider (left from an observer on the shore).

pool board. A generally wider skateboard, after the ones preferred in the early 1980s.

POP Pier. Pronounced "pee-oh-pee," according to Wikipedia. *What's in a name?* You can't make this stuff up. See Pacific Ocean Park, above.

popsicle board. The most common skateboard in use today, of a symmetrical uniform size and shape with a double-ended kicktail.

P.O.S. Acronym for "piece of shit."

pump track. Usually made of asphalt, it's a skatepark set up like a BMX course—featuring banks and bumps and opposed to street or vert.

Rampage Ramp. The first complete half-pipe ramp ever made. At eighteen feet in diameter, it was modeled after the Mount Baldy spillway.

RAND Corporation. RAND Corporation is an American nonprofit global policy think tank originally formed by Douglas Aircraft Company to offer research and analysis to the armed forces.

Randy & Larry. Anonyms for our pilot and co-pilot on the day we crashed. Randy was indeed a military pilot right out of the Vietnam War. The personal details of co-pilot Larry I'm fuzzy on. All of the events and dialogue are accurate.

razor clams. Pacific razor clams have an elongated oblong narrow shell, ranging from three to six inches in length in the southern portion of its range, with individuals up to eleven inches.

Rhino Racing. A couple of skaters specializing in catamaran-style riding and racing of skateboards. They were also members of the cover band Bratz.

Rift, the. My name for easy access to the fun feeling that occurs when executing banked turns.

Rockwell, Marshall "Tom." Mathematician, physician, partner in Sparks Inc.

royal jelly. A honey bee secretion that is used in the nutrition of larvae, as well as adult queens. It is secreted from the glands of worker bees. A special, exotic nourishment.

Ryan, Tommy. A fast and stylish racer, TR was a mainstay of the Turner Racing team.

Schufeldt, Denis. The first and original skateboard speed racer. He worked at the Bahne factory and stepped into the role as test pilot for Bahne/Cadillac. Denis went really fast on equipment that today would be considered extremely dangerous: crimped steel trucks and loose-bearing wheels.

Self Realization Fellowship (**SRF**). A worldwide spiritual organization founded by Paramahansa Yogananda in 1920 to serve as Yogananda's instrument for the preservation and worldwide dissemination of his writings and teachings, including Kriya Yoga. His book *Autobiography of a Yogi*, published in 1946, is still in print. Everyone should go to Amazon.com right now and buy a copy, then practice Kriya Yoga; the world would be a better place.

sensei. A martial arts teacher or master.

Shadmore Woods. The area of preserved woods in between the town of Montauk and Ditch Plains in Montauk, New York.

Sheridan, Don. Surfer/skater from Long Beach, California. He was a skateshop owner and advertising designer.

Sherman, Brig. Scientist, inventor and Steve Sherman's dad. Brig would develop the earliest electronic timing systems for the Sunday races at La Costa. He really classed up our act.

Sherman, Steve. Among the younger members of the La Costa boys, Steve showed early promise by winning local races. Too young to drive, he'd come with his father, scientist Brig Sherman. Steve grew up to become a successful surf photographer. Also known as T-Sherm.

shred heads. Dedicated skaters, surfers or snowboarders.

single ski. Or monoski, boots are fixed on one wide ski. Predecessor to the snowboard.

SkateBoarder Magazine. The magazine was first published in 1964–65 as a quarterly. It was resurrected in 1975 around the photography and vision of editor Warren Bolster. It folded again in the early 1980s and was resurrected with annual issues in 1997–98, had limited success thereafter and closed again for good in 2013.

skatepark. A skateboard park. A recreational environment made for skateboarding and other rolling vehicles.

Skatetopia. One of the first, full-featured skateparks ever built, with a pro shop and full amenities, it featured the first concrete half-pipe ever built.

skog. Long-distance skateboarding for exercise, a mash-up of the words skating and jogging.

Skoldberg, Bob. Slalom racer and longtime Hobie team member Bobby was a great racer and something of a partner to Henry Hester. He was a giant slalom specialist and very hard to beat on those courses.

Skunkworks. A *skunkworks project* is a project typically developed by a small and loosely structured group of people who research and develop a project primarily for the sake of innovation. Derived from Lockheed Martin company's Advanced Development Projects division.

sled. Another name for a skateboard or surfboard.

Smith, Lance. An original La Costa boy, Lance is a writer, photographer, skater and surfer. He was fundamental to the beginnings of skateboarding at the Sunday Races at La Costa and wrote and shot photos for *SkateBoarder* and the *National Skateboard Review*.

Smithsonian Institution. Nicknamed "the nation's attic," it is located primarily in Washington, D.C. The institute consists of nineteen museums and nine research centers.

Snurfer. A predecessor of the snowboard. It was a mono ski, ridden like a snowboard, but like a skateboard or surfboard, it had no binding.

starboard. A nautical term for the right-hand side of a vessel when facing forward.

Stecyk, Craig. Photographer, writer, artist. He is singlehandedly responsible for launching the Z-Boys phenomenon.

St. Pierre, Paul. Coach of Team Bahne. He had a sharp eye for talent and recruited.

surfboard shaper. The person who sculpts the board into its final, optimal shape. In modern times, a portion of this job is sometimes done by a computer-driven machine.

Surfer Publications. A group of high-quality magazines that focus on travel and gravity sports. The anchor publication is *Surfer Magazine*, known as "the bible of the sport."

Swami's. Also known as "Swami's Reef," an internationally known surf spot located in Encinitas, California. Swami's was named after Swami Paramahansa Yogananda because the grounds of the hermitage overlook the reef point.

Tate Modern. An art gallery of modern art and forms located in London, England.

Tholl, Peter. A fast and stylish slalom racer and member of the Logan team, Peter was among the younger members of the La Costa boys.

Thornhill, Laura. An original member of the Logan Earth Ski team, Thornhill was a great slalom and freestyle skater and moved effortlessly to pools and pipes and bowls. She was the first woman skater to ever have a signature skateboard model.

Tracker Trucks. The first skateboard truck built with the future of the sport in mind—sturdy and maneuverable beyond the performance needs of the day. The sport quickly grew into the performance and safety that they provided.

Trans-Alaska Pipeline (TAPS). At over eight hundred miles, one of the world's largest pipeline systems. It is commonly called the Alaska Pipeline. The pipeline was built between 1974 and 1977 after the 1973 oil crisis.

trucks. These are the metal turning devices on skateboards as well as roller skates. They come in various widths.

T-Sherm. Professional surf photographer and grownup alter ego of slalom racer Steve Sherman.

turnbuckle. A device for adjusting the tension or length of ropes or cables. It normally consists of two threaded eye bolts screwed into each end of a small metal frame. The tension can be adjusted by rotating the frame, which causes both eye bolts to be screwed in or out simultaneously, without twisting the eye bolts or attached cables.

Turner, Bobby. From La Jolla, California, Bobby was an innovative craftsman and designer. His Turner SummerSki slalom skateboards and his Turner racing team were built around Bobby's vision and skateboard design.

Turner SummerSki. These skateboards were a breakthrough in slalom skateboard design, constructed like surfboards and certain snow skis. They revolutionized slalom racing and board design; some of the best contemporary slalom racing boards are still made the same way.

Upland Skatepark. Also the Upland Pipeline. The first commercial skatepark to incorporate a full pipe into its features. It was a grand place.

vert. Vertical skating, that is, in pools, pipes and bowls.

vig. Slang for a charge taken on bets by a bookie or gambling establishment or mobsters. Interest on a loan shark's loan.

Weaver, Gregg. Also known as the Cadillac Kid while riding for Bahne/Cadillac. Gregg was the sport's original icon known for his impeccable style and grace. He later skated for the Hobie team.

Wilkens, Steve. Action photographer who worked for *Surfer Magazine*, among others, beginning in the 1960s. Mentor to Warren Bolster.

Williams, Michael. Surfer, slalom racer, inventor and Turner SummerSki team member, Mike designed the Gullwing Truck, innovative in its day, with a reverse kingpin design that has since been widely adopted for cruiser boards and racing boards. Michael currently pursues a shamanic life.

winch. A mechanical device that is used to pull in or let out or otherwise adjust the tension of a rope or cable.

Winnebago. An American-made motor home.

Yandall, Chris. Perennially stoked lifelong skater Chris was among the original La Costa crew. He was a great slalom racer and invented several iconic skateboard tricks. He founded skogging, an aerobic approach to long-distance skateboarding.

Yugo. A Yugoslavian automobile that is remembered as the worst car ever made.

Z-Boys skaters, or **Zephyr Team**. Built around Jeff Ho's Z-Flex Skateboards, the Z-Boys represented the shop and and came to prominence at the skateboard contest held during the Bahne/Cadillac Oceanfest at the Del Mar Fairgrounds. Earliest members included Bob Biniak, Paul Constantineau, Jim Muir, Peggy Oki, Shogo Kubo and Wentzle Ruml IV, Stacy Peralta, Jay Adams and Tony Alva.

Z-Flex. Skateboards made by Jeff Ho from the Zephyr Surfboards and ridden by the Zephyr skateboard team.

Me, co-director of the Cow Palace
contest, 1976. *Warren Bolster.*

ABOUT THE AUTHOR

John O'Malley was part of the original Encinitas, California Skunkworks crew. Along with his partner, Jack Graham, John created the first skateparks.

He is a multimedia designer and says that he writes only when it's absolutely necessary.

Visit us at
www.historypress.com